AKHYAYIKAS IV

100 HILARIOUS PARABLES TO INSTILL WISDOM THROUGH WIT

AKHYAYIKAS IV

100 HILARIOUS PARABLES TO INSTILL WISDOM THROUGH WIT

RAJESH SESHADRI

PAPER TOWNS
PUBLISHERS

PAPER TOWNS
PUBLISHERS

First published by 2025

Papertowns Publishers
72, Vishwanath Dham Colony,
Niwaru Road, Jhotwara,
Jaipur, 302012

Akhyayikas IV

ISBN Print Book – 978-93-6185-599-3

Printed in India

CONTENTS

PREFACE

Stories are more than mere entertainment—they are living vessels that reach deep into the subconscious mind, planting seeds of insight, change, and wisdom. As Carl Jung famously noted, "*Until you make the unconscious conscious, it will direct your life, and you will call it fate.*" Parables, folktales, and anecdotes bypass the barrier of logic and speak directly to the heart, reshaping beliefs quietly yet powerfully. They create emotional hooks that linger long after the page is closed.

Humour, in particular, makes this journey enjoyable. Neuroscience tells us that laughter activates the brain's *dopamine reward system*, enhancing motivation and long-term memory retention—essential ingredients for true learning[1]. In light-hearted moments, we are more open, receptive, and willing to explore ideas that might confront our assumptions. The *surprise twist* in a joke engages our minds, grabs our attention, and lodges key messages more firmly.

Research in educational psychology supports this: appropriately placed humour improves retention, reduces anxiety, strengthens social bonds, and fosters a positive learning environment[2]. Yet, as studies caution, humour must be *relevant and respectful* of the story's deeper intention to truly support learning[3].

---

1 https://www.edutopia.org/blog/laughter-learning-humor-boosts-retention-sarah-henderson?utm_source=chatgpt.com "Laughter and Learning: Humor Boosts Retention - Edutopia"

2 https://www.frontiersin.org/journals/psychology/articles/10.3389/fpsyg.2025.1445362/full?utm_source=chatgpt.com "Teaching and learning with instructional humor: a review of five ..."

3 https://storytimeaiapp.com/blog/importance-of-funny-story-humor-supports-childhood-learning/?utm_source=chatgpt.com "The importance of a funny story: how humor supports childhood ..."

Enter Mulla Nasruddin: the timeless *wise fool* whose simple wit bears elegant twists and universal lessons. Rooted in Islamic–Middle Eastern folklore, Nasruddin appears in thousands of anecdotes that balance levity with layers of meaning. His tales—like the one where he returns to the courtyard to look for a ring, simply because the light is better there—mix absurdity with wisdom in a single snapshot[4].

In this, the fourth book of the Akhyayikas series, we bring you a hundred short stories that aim to humorously disrupt daily thought patterns: the illogical logic of society, the subtle prejudices we carry, the small absurdities we overlook. Each tale offers a moment of laughter—and with it, a chance to pause, reflect, and reconsider.

Humour acts as a bridge—drawing you close with a laugh, then guiding you on a journey of introspection. It lowers mental defences, so when the wisdom arrives, it is embraced more willingly. The subconscious is not *rational*, but it responds to emotion and repetition—and humour delivers both. As described by relief theory, humour safely *releases tension*, helping us see with fresh perspective and absorb new insights.

This *curated* collection is crafted for curious minds, seekers of wisdom, story-lovers, and those who appreciate that the most profound lessons often come wrapped in a jest. Engaging, concise, and rich with meaning, these stories honour the tradition of ***Akhyayikas***—narratives that inspire, coach, teach, and motivate.

May these tales of Mulla Nasruddin make you laugh, ponder, smile—and perhaps carry a little sage wisdom into your everyday life.

4 https://en.wikipedia.org/wiki/Theories_of_humor?utm_source=chatgpt.com "Theories of humor"

INTRODUCTION

These stories that you are about to read do not belong to me. They belong to the vast and timeless spiritual heritage of humanity—gathered across borders, generations, and belief systems. My role, at best, has been that of a tailor and seamstress: cutting, stitching, adjusting the seams, and occasionally adding embellishments. The credit for the cloth, the thread, the design of the fabric, and even the original stitchwork lies elsewhere. The stories themselves have been inherited from the open treasury of folklore, oral traditions, and spiritual satire passed down from wise storytellers whose names are often lost to time. The only liberties I have taken are those of language, structure, tone, and occasionally, brevity or elaboration—solely for your reading pleasure and introspective benefit.

Mulla Nasruddin, the central character of this book, is an everyman and a no-man. He is both foolish and wise, ignorant and awakened, materialistic and spiritual. His tales are absurd and deeply meaningful, ridiculous and revelatory, hilarious and hauntingly honest. He mirrors the contradictions within us, the hypocrisies we justify, and the truths we are too afraid to name aloud. That is the reason these tales persist across centuries and civilizations. One finds versions of Nasruddin (or Nasreddin, Juha, Goha, or Hoja) in Persia, Turkey, India, Arabia, Central Asia, and North Africa. His jokes are told in coffee shops and classrooms, in psychology lectures and Sufi circles, by illiterate villagers and eminent scholars alike.

As with all stories in the Akhyayikas series, the intent is never just to entertain. The intention is to gently provoke insight, trigger reflection, and inspire subtle transformation. The humour, wit, or satire is but the sugar coating to help the wisdom go down with ease. And yet, it is precisely this humour that often disarms our conditioned resistance to uncomfortable truths. We are more likely to laugh at a version of ourselves in Mulla Nasruddin, than to accept the same message if it came cloaked in solemn sermonising or abstract philosophy.

In my previous volume—*Akhyayikas III: 100 Insightful Zen Stories That Provoke Introspection*—many of you shared appreciative feedback and found the parables enlightening. However, one consistent note that emerged from several readers was the desire for a little more scaffolding—an accompanying commentary or explanation after each story. My original intent was to let the stories breathe freely, encouraging readers to sit with the parable, chew on its meaning, and allow their own inner wisdom to surface. And that, in my view, remains a powerful approach.

However, I understand that for many readers, especially those not habituated to the Zen or Sufi way of *holding paradox*, some guidance can act as a catalyst for deeper introspection. In this volume, therefore, I have responded to your requests. Each of the hundred stories is followed by a commentary—brief, unpretentious, and free of academic jargon. These are not exhaustive interpretations, nor are they meant to be taken as the *correct* reading. Instead, think of them as sparks—initiators of dialogue between your conscious and subconscious selves. They are like hints in a crossword puzzle: they do not give away the answer, but they help you reach it in your own time.

Another wonderful aspect of this book is its nonlinear structure. You do not need to start at the beginning and plod through it sequentially. Much like how life rarely presents its lessons in a structured syllabus, *you are invited to open any page and start there*. Choose instinctively, randomly, or with focused intent—whatever your inner voice suggests. The right story tends to find the right reader at the right moment.

> *However, I offer one piece of sincere advice: do not binge-read. Resist the urge to consume multiple stories in one sitting, as though ticking off items on a checklist. These stories are not fast food; they are more like vintage wine or a well-brewed filter coffee—best sipped slowly, with pauses for silence. Ideally, read no more than one or two stories at a time. Once you finish a story, spend at least thirty minutes letting it linger in your mind. Don't rush to understand it or to categorize it as spiritual, funny, profound, or mundane. Just sit with it. Ask yourself what message it might hold for you in this moment of your life. Is it challenging an assumption? Is it revealing a blind spot? Is it mocking an aspect of yourself that needs to be laughed at before it can be healed?*

These stories operate on multiple levels. Sometimes the meaning is immediately obvious; it lands like an arrow straight to your heart or funny bone. At other times, the story hangs in the background of your consciousness like a puzzle yet unsolved. And then, one day, while washing dishes or walking through a quiet street, the insight dawns—unexpectedly, unforced, and utterly transformative. That is the beauty of the storytelling tradition Nasruddin belongs to: its truths are not imposed but revealed through osmosis.

In fact, you may discover that a story which didn't seem to work for you the first time, suddenly offers a fresh insight when you revisit it after weeks, months, or even years. The stories remain the same; it is you who evolves. And thus, what was once opaque becomes luminous. What was once hilarious becomes hauntingly honest. What was once nonsensical suddenly sounds like your own inner voice whispering to you from the page.

These stories also transcend religious boundaries. They are not limited to any one dogma or deity. Mulla Nasruddin, after all, has been claimed and adopted by Muslims, Hindus, Christians, Sufis, secularists, atheists, mystics, and modern psychologists alike. His stories reveal the universal absurdity of the human condition—our greed, our pride, our fear, our misplaced certainty—and they also celebrate our boundless capacity for love, curiosity, self-awareness, and laughter.

Whether you are a seeker on the spiritual path, a lover of storytelling, a fan of satire, or simply someone who appreciates wit with wisdom, this book is for you. The Akhyayikas series is not a sermon or a syllabus. It is a companion—amusing, annoying, honest, and at times disconcerting. Like Nasruddin himself, it never claims to know more than you. It merely nudges you toward remembering what you may have forgotten.

Each tale is like a mirror, a jester, and a lantern rolled into one. Sometimes the mirror reflects your own folly. Sometimes the jester teases your ego. Sometimes the lantern lights up an inner corridor you had not dared to explore. Whatever happens, you are changed—sometimes imperceptibly, sometimes irreversibly.

Read slowly. Reflect often. Laugh loudly. And most importantly, enjoy the journey. It may not offer you answers, but it will leave you asking the right questions.

Welcome, then, to the delightful world of Mulla Nasruddin—where the truths are hidden in plain sight, and the jokes are often just a shade away from divine revelation.

ABOUT THE AUTHOR

Rajesh Seshadri is a storyteller, coach, strategist, and seeker—someone who has worn many hats, but always with a single-minded pursuit: to understand and elevate the human experience.

With nearly three decades of leadership across the volatile, high-stakes world of corporate India, Rajesh has journeyed from the trenches to the C-suite, acquiring a deep and nuanced understanding of people, performance, and purpose. His professional arc, documented in part on his LinkedIn profile, reflects a rare combination of strategic vision and emotional intelligence—qualities that also inform his work as a writer and coach.

Rajesh is a Fellow Member of the ICAI (FCMA) and holds dual Post Graduate Diplomas in Finance and Human Resource Management. He is also a Certified Leadership Coach, Life Coach, and a trained therapist with credentials in Clinical Hypnotherapy, Gestalt Therapy, and the Silva UltraMind System. A member of esteemed bodies like the APA, AAH, ISTD, AIMA, and BMA, Rajesh continues to be a bridge between the rational and the intuitive, the scientific and the spiritual.

In coaching rooms, classrooms, and corporate boardrooms, Rajesh often turns to the power of storytelling. For him, stories are more than just tools—they are vessels of wisdom, mirrors of human folly, and sparks for transformation. His unique blend of psychological depth and corporate pragmatism gives him the ability to draw profound insights from the simplest of tales.

Akhyayikas IV – 100 Hilarious Parables to Instil Wisdom Through Wit is part of Rajesh's ongoing exploration into how wit, wisdom, and wonder can be compressed into the economy of a single anecdote. Mulla Nasruddin—foolish and wise, ridiculous and sublime—serves as the perfect conduit for truths too delicate for lecture and too potent for dogma. With each parable, Rajesh invites the reader not merely to laugh, but to look closer, reflect deeper, and emerge a little wiser.

Having previously authored *Threads of Reality* and *Akhyayikas III – 100 Insightful Zen Stories That Provoke Introspection*, Rajesh's work continues to reflect his core belief: that humour, insight, and a well-placed question can open doors that logic alone cannot. This book is not just a collection of Nasruddin stories—it is a curated experience, lovingly reinterpreted and richly annotated, where every tale is followed by commentary that nudges the reader gently toward self-reflection and perspective.

Rajesh continues to write, coach, and lead from a space of curiosity and compassion—believing that transformation, whether personal or professional, begins with a story well told.

OTHER BOOKS BY THE AUTHOR

Breaking Free from the MAFA Syndrome[5]
How to Stay Focused and Enhance Personal Productivity to Accelerate Your Growth

Akhyayikas I[6]
100 Short Stories and Anecdotes that Inspire, Coach, Teach and Motivate

Akhyayikas II[7]
100 Extraordinary Feats of Ordinary People Who Dared to Dream

Akhyayikas III[8]
100 Insightful Zen Stories That Provoke Introspection

Threads of Reality[9]
Unravelling India's Deepest Mysteries

---

[5] https://amzn.to/3GscMmr
[6] https://amzn.to/3YTbHeu
[7] https://amzn.to/3WWvyb6
[8] https://amzn.to/42dKuUU
[9] https://amzn.to/46WwRil

"Brief stories and parables work their way into the subconscious and activate its hidden forces."

— Idries Shah on Mulla Nasruddin tales

1

THE INVISIBLE CARGO

Nasruddin approached the border yet again, leading a tired-looking donkey loaded with bundles of straw. The border inspector, sharp-eyed and suspicious, raised his hand.

"Halt! What's your business today?"

"I am but an honest smuggler," said Nasruddin with a straight face.

The inspector narrowed his eyes. "Is that so? Then let me inspect those bundles. You will be prosecuted or fined in case we find any contraband."

"As you wish," Nasruddin replied nonchalantly.

The inspector tore through the straw, strand by strand. He sniffed, poked, pulled, and even shook the bundles. Nothing. Frustrated, he waved Nasruddin through.

But the next day, there he was again—same donkey, same straw bundles.

The inspector doubled down. He searched Nasruddin's clothes, his shoes, even the donkey's harness and tail. Still, nothing.

Day after day, year after year, Nasruddin came through with his straw-carrying donkey. And day after day, the inspector found nothing—though he couldn't help but notice how Nasruddin's robes grew richer, his turban more elaborate, and his rings more numerous.

Eventually, the inspector retired, still haunted by the mystery.

One afternoon, years later, he spotted a familiar face in the marketplace. "Nasruddin!" he called out, grabbing the old trickster's arm. "You *must* tell me. I'm no longer on duty, so you will not get into trouble. Please—what were you smuggling all those years?"

Nasruddin leaned in with a smile and whispered, "Donkeys."

Commentary: The Art of Looking Without Seeing

This classic tale is a brilliant commentary on the human tendency to overlook the obvious while obsessing over the obscure. The border inspector, trained to look for contraband in the usual places—bags, clothes, compartments—was so focused on the *concealed* that he missed what was *in plain sight.*

The lesson is profound yet humorous: Sometimes, we miss life's truths not because they are hidden, but because they're *too obvious to notice.* Our filters, biases, and expectations often blind us to reality, making us search for answers where they aren't—while the truth stands quietly beside us, disguised as the mundane.

Nasruddin's genius lies in how he uses the inspector's assumptions against him. He never lies. He does not hide anything. He simply lets the inspector's tunnel vision do the work.

In leadership, relationships, and personal growth, this story reminds us to ask:

- What *donkeys* are we failing to see in our lives?
- Where are we *complicating* what might be startlingly simple?
- Are we focusing so hard on the details that we have lost sight of the *big picture*?

In true Nasruddin fashion, the laugh comes first—and the lesson lingers long after.

2

AIMING FOR THE WRONG TARGET

One lively evening at the village teahouse, Mulla Nasruddin stood up, eyes twinkling with mischief.

"I'll bet ten coins I can fire thirty shots from 200 yards and call every one correctly before the marker signals a thing! Who dares take the wager?"

A curious stranger smirked. "You are on!"

They marched to the shooting range. Nasruddin took aim at the open field—nowhere near the target—and fired.

"Miss!" he declared confidently.

Another shot. "Miss!"

And another. "Miss again!"

The stranger's eyebrows shot up. "Wait a minute! You are not even aiming at the target. You have missed three times in a row!"

Nasruddin nodded. "Exactly as I said. I promised to call every shot—and I have been right every time. I am not aiming for the target… I am aiming for your ten-spot."

Commentary: Precision Without Purpose Is Just Noise

Nasruddin's tale is a masterclass in the *deceptive dance of semantics*. While the words are technically accurate, the intent is cleverly misdirected. This story humorously exposes the gap between *performance and purpose*, and between *results and real value*.

Many people—especially in bureaucracies, academia, or even business—become obsessed with **metrics, output, or clever wordplay**, forgetting the real objective. They hit all their *marks* without ever asking whether they were aiming at the right target.

The story urges us to reflect:

- Are we just staying busy, or are we being *purposeful*?
- Are we setting goals that are *meaningful*—or just winnable?
- Are we honouring the spirit of a *commitment*, or hiding behind the letter?

In the end, Mulla Nasruddin wins the bet—but teaches a lesson far richer than the prize: *Even perfect execution is useless if you aim at the wrong thing.*

3

THE GEOGRAPHY OF PREJUDICE

The teacher, determined to broaden the narrow worldviews of her students, gave them a thoughtful assignment.

"I want each of you to write an essay on your views of foreigners," she announced.

The next day, she collected the essays. Most were naive but tolerable attempts—except for one. Young Nasruddin had turned in a sheet with just one line:

"All foreigners are bastards."

The class gasped. The teacher, holding back her fury, said nothing. Instead, she returned the essays and planned her next move.

At the next lecture, she launched into a vivid exploration of global culture. She spoke passionately about Greek architecture, Roman law, English theatre, German music, Italian poetry, Russian literature, Chinese philosophy, and African art.

Then she said gently, "Now, please rewrite your essays on foreigners."

The class set to work, visibly transformed by the lecture. Later, she eagerly picked up Nasruddin's new submission and read it aloud, hoping for a changed heart.

It read:

"All foreigners are bastards. Some are cunning bastards."

Commentary: When Minds Resist Expansion

This story, sharp as a scalpel, slices straight into the *resilience of prejudice*. Nasruddin's essay is not simply a joke—it is a reflection of how deeply-rooted beliefs can cling, even in the face of overwhelming evidence or education.

Despite the teacher's best efforts—an elegant display of the world's cultural riches—Nasruddin does not revise his worldview. He reinforces it with even greater conviction and nuance.

This tale is darkly comic, but its insight is hauntingly real:

- Facts alone *cannot* transform beliefs.
- Exposure to culture *does not* guarantee openness.
- Some people listen only to *reinforce* what they already believe.

The humour lies in Nasruddin's deadpan delivery and refusal to budge. But the lesson is deeply relevant, especially in an age of echo chambers and ideological rigidity.

In essence, this parable is a reminder that *teaching is not the same as transforming*—and that sometimes, laughter is the only way to cope with the stubbornness of the human mind.

4

THE IDIOT WHO OUTSMARTED EVERYONE

Every market day, Mulla Nasruddin would stand in the street, quietly attracting a crowd. The ritual was always the same: someone would offer him a large coin and a small one. And each time, Nasruddin would unflinchingly take the smaller coin.

Onlookers laughed. Children pointed. "Poor fool," they'd say. "Doesn't even know the value of money!"

One afternoon, a kind-hearted gentleman took Nasruddin aside and whispered, "Mulla, you should take the bigger coin. It is worth ten times more. Why let people mock you like this?"

Nasruddin smiled. "Ah, but if I ever take the larger coin, the game ends. They will stop offering me money to prove I am more foolish than they are. As long as they think I am the idiot, the coins keep coming."

Later that day, as Nasruddin stepped out of the mosque after prayers, a beggar called out for alms.

"Tell me," Nasruddin asked, "Are you extravagant?"

"Yes, Nasruddin," the beggar replied.

"Do you enjoy sitting at cafés, sipping coffee, smoking, and visiting the public baths?"

"Very much."

"And do you sometimes indulge with friends over drinks?"

"Of course," said the beggar.

Nasruddin nodded and handed him a gold coin.

A few steps later, another beggar approached, having overheard the exchange.

"Are you extravagant?" Nasruddin asked.

"No, sir," the man replied proudly.

"Do you drink coffee? Smoke? Go to the baths?"

"No. I live simply and pray constantly."

Nasruddin reached into his pouch and gave him a single copper coin.

The beggar looked at the coin, aghast. "Why, Mulla? Why such a small amount for a pious man like me, and a fortune for a hedonist?"

Nasruddin smiled gently. "Because his needs, my friend, are far greater than yours."

Commentary: The Fool Who Knew the Score

These tales show Mulla Nasruddin at his finest—misunderstood, underestimated, and several steps ahead of the crowd.

In the first story, he plays the fool to expose the real foolishness of those obsessed with appearances. He reminds us of a powerful truth: sometimes the smartest move is to let others *think* they are smarter. Pride makes people act predictably—and Nasruddin capitalizes on it with calm cunning.

The second parable challenges our assumptions about fairness. Nasruddin does not give based on virtue or austerity. He gives based on *need*—a subtle but compassionate twist. The one who squanders has more *requirements* while the frugal man, by his own admission, needs little to survive.

Together, these stories challenge conventional morality, question the meaning of wisdom, and delight us with their sly subversion.

As always, in Nasruddin's world, the laugh is just the doorway—what lies beyond is deeper than it first appears.

5

WHEN THE DONKEY SPOKE TOO SOON

One hot afternoon, a neighbour—one Nasruddin wasn't particularly fond of—wandered into his compound.

"Mullah," the neighbour said sweetly, "may I borrow your donkey for a few hours? I need to haul some grain to the mill."

Nasruddin, quick on his feet and quicker with excuses, replied, "Ah, I would love to help, but just yesterday my brother came from the next town and took the donkey for that very task. Poor fellow's not here."

Disappointed but polite, the neighbour thanked him and turned to leave.

Just then, from the back of the compound, the donkey let out a loud and unmistakable bray.

The neighbour spun around. "Mullah Sahib," he said incredulously, "did you not just say the donkey wasn't here?"

Without missing a beat, Nasruddin smiled and asked, "My dear friend, who are you going to believe—*me* or a donkey?"

Commentary: Truth, Lies, and the Art of Evasion

At first glance, this story is pure slapstick—classic Nasruddin cheek. But behind the laugh lies a sharp commentary on *human denial, manipulation, and the elasticity of truth.*

When caught in a lie, most people scramble to justify or shift blame. Nasruddin, instead, chooses the outrageous: he doubles down on the absurd and asks a question that forces the listener to question their own logic.

It's a brilliant illustration of:

- *Cognitive dissonance*: How people react when presented with conflicting information.
- *Authority vs. evidence*: Many trust credible voices over obvious facts, even when the truth is braying in their backyard.
- *Gaslighting:* A subtle jab at how people in power—or with clever words—can deny reality and still keep a straight face.

The humour, as always, is the bait. The real lesson? *Beware of those who lie so confidently that they make you question your ears—even when it is the donkey who told the truth.*

6

THE ETHICS OF STEAK

A traveling scholar invited Mulla Nasruddin to join him for dinner at a local restaurant.

The scholar, seeking to impress, ordered two fine lamb steaks.

After a short wait, the waiter returned with a platter holding two pieces—one noticeably larger than the other.

Without hesitation, Nasruddin reached out and took the bigger steak for himself.

The scholar's jaw dropped. "Mullah!" he cried, appalled. "What you've done is against every moral, ethical, spiritual, and cultural principle! Don't you know anything about manners? Humility? Self-sacrifice? What kind of person just grabs the larger portion for himself?"

Nasruddin listened calmly through the long lecture. When the scholar finally paused for breath, the Mullah asked, "And what would *you* have done in my place?"

The scholar puffed up proudly. "I would have taken the smaller steak, of course."

Nasruddin smiled and slid the smaller steak onto the scholar's plate. "Well then—there you go. Enjoy!"

Commentary: Virtue, Vanity, and the Illusion of Selflessness

This story is a masterstroke in exposing performative virtue. The scholar, disguised in the language of ethics and etiquette, pretends that his outrage is not about justice or fairness—but about not being the one who got the smaller piece.

Nasruddin's response is devastatingly simple and utterly effective. By giving the scholar exactly what he claimed he would have chosen, Nasruddin:

- Unmasks *hypocrisy* hiding behind moral grandstanding,
- Shows how *expectations of others' sacrifice* often mask our own desire to benefit,
- And humorously reveals that sometimes true fairness lies not in preaching, but in giving people exactly what they ask for.

This tale reminds us that *righteousness, when used to shame others, often masks hidden pride*. And in true Nasruddin fashion, the lesson is delivered not with fury or fire—but with a fork and a smile.

Bon appétit, indeed.

7

THE COLOUR OF CAUTION

One fine morning, the village barber was summoned to the mayor's palace to trim His Excellency's beard.

As he neared the end of his careful work, the barber casually remarked, "Your beard, sir, is beginning to show signs of gray."

The mayor's eyes narrowed. "GRAY?!" he roared. "How dare you insult me like that! Guards—jail him for one year!"

Shaking with anger, the mayor turned to a nearby attendant. "Do *you* see any gray in my beard?"

The man hesitated. "Almost none at all, Your Excellency."

"Almost?" the mayor bellowed. "Guards—two years in jail for this traitor!"

He turned to another attendant. "What about you?"

The man bowed low. "Sir, your beard is a magnificent black, dark as the feathers of a raven."

The mayor glared. "Liar! Guards—ten lashes and three years in prison for him!"

Then he turned to Nasruddin, who had been watching silently from the corner.

"Mulla," he growled, "tell me—what colour is my beard?"

Nasruddin folded his hands respectfully and replied, "Your Excellency, I am afraid I was born colour-blind, and therefore not qualified to answer such a delicate question."

Commentary: When Truth Is a Dangerous Game

This tale is a timeless parable about the *perils of power, the unpredictability of tyrants, and the art of self-preservation* in an irrational world.

Everyone in the story is punished—not for telling the truth or lying, but for speaking at all. The mayor isn't seeking honesty or praise; he's seeking *validation of his ego* and punishing anyone who doesn't navigate his whims perfectly.

Enter Nasruddin, who plays neither the sycophant nor the truth-teller. Instead, he uses wit to sidestep the trap entirely. His response, humorous on the surface, is a deep lesson in survival: *When reason is futile and tyranny reigns, silence—or strategic ambiguity—may be the wisest form of speech.*

This story resonates in any context where authority demands not truth, but flattery. It reminds us that sometimes, the only winning move is to *not play the game at all.*

8

THE BRIGHT SIDE OF BULLET HOLES

Mulla Nasruddin was infamous in his circle of friends—not for his mischief or his madness, but for his maddening optimism. No matter how bleak the news, he would always nod wisely and say:

"It could have been worse."

One evening at the club, his friends decided they'd had enough. They conspired to present him with a situation so horrendous, so utterly devoid of silver linings, that even the eternally cheerful Mulla would be speechless.

Over drinks, one of them leaned in and said gravely, "Mulla, did you hear about poor George? He came home last night, found his wife in bed with another man... He shot them both—and then shot himself."

Mulla took a long, thoughtful sip of tea and nodded. "Terrible... truly terrible. But" he added, "it could have been worse."

His friend slammed his glass down. "Worse?! How could it *possibly* have been worse?!"

Nasruddin leaned closer and whispered, "Well, if it had happened *the night before*, I would be dead now."

Commentary: Optimism or Opportunism?

This darkly comic tale straddles the line between humour and horror and delivers a sharp jab at both toxic positivity and self-centered survivalism.

Nasruddin's catchphrase, "*It could have been worse,*" usually signals hopeful detachment from life's misfortunes. But here, he flips it into a personal escape clause—revealing that his optimism is not so much moral as it is practical, even selfish.

This story highlights:

- The *absurdity of relentless optimism*, especially when it overlooks real suffering.
- The *power of perspective*—how one event can be a tragedy for one and a near-miss for another.
- And most of all, Nasruddin's *uncanny ability* to deflect any situation back into his own bizarre logic of survival.

It is a reminder that humour, even when uncomfortable, can be a tool for coping—but also a mirror reflecting the narrow lens of self-interest through which we often see the world.

In classic Nasruddin style, he survives—*not because he avoids trouble, but because he always sees himself just one step away from it.*

9

THE TIP-OFF

One chilly afternoon, Mulla Nasruddin arrived at the local bathhouse clad in tattered robes and dusty sandals.

Seeing his shabby appearance, the bath attendant barely acknowledged him. No warm greetings. No courteous service. Just a half-hearted towel toss.

Nasruddin bathed quietly, and when he was done, to everyone's surprise, he handed the attendant a hefty tip with a generous smile.

A week later, he returned—this time dressed in a fine robe, shoes polished, and turban spotless.

The same attendant rushed over, nearly stumbling over himself in his eagerness. Hot water, fragrant oils, the softest towels—Nasruddin was pampered like a visiting sultan.

But when it came time to tip, the Mulla reached into his pouch and flicked the man a single dime. He added a pointed scowl for good measure.

The attendant looked stunned. "But… but Mulla… last week you gave me—"

Nasruddin raised a hand. "That tip was for today's treatment. Today's tip is for last week's service."

Commentary: Value, Prejudice, and the Price of Assumptions

This story is a brilliant reflection of how we judge others based on appearances, and how often *kindness is conditional*—reserved only for those we assume are worth it.

The bath attendant, like many of us, equated worn clothes with worthlessness, and fine garments with generosity. His service was based not on *ethics or duty*, but on *expectation and calculation.*

Nasruddin's tipping strategy flips the script with poetic justice. He rewards the man *before* he earns it—and penalizes him *after* he tries to manipulate the outcome.

The message is clear:

- Do not judge a book—or a bather—by its cover.
- Genuine service should not be influenced by appearances.
- And most importantly: the past has a way of showing up when you least expect it—*sometimes in the form of a tiny tip.*

In classic Nasruddin fashion, the lesson is served with a side of wit—and a splash of very cold water.

10

FATE, OR JUST A BAD ASSUMPTION?

A curious seeker once asked Mulla Nasruddin, "Mulla, what exactly is fate?"

Nasruddin didn't blink. "Assumptions," he said.

"Assumptions?" the man repeated, puzzled. "In what way?"

"Well," Nasruddin began, stroking his beard, "You assume things will go well—and they don't. You call that bad luck. You assume things will go terribly—and they don't. That is good luck. You assume some things will happen, and others will not—and when life surprises you, you say it was Fate. The truth is: you assumed... and you were wrong."

He paused, then added, "You assume the future is unknowable. When your assumptions collapse, you call it destiny."

Commentary: The Fallacy of Forecasting

This brief but profound dialogue reveals Nasruddin at his philosophical best. It turns the conventional understanding of *fate* on its head—suggesting that what we often call fate is nothing more than *misplaced expectation or lack of awareness.*

We often:

- Blame fate when plans fail.
- Praise fate when they succeed unexpectedly.
- Curse fate when we are blindsided. But what if fate isn't some invisible cosmic script? *What if it is simply the gap between what we expect and what is?*

Nasruddin's answer challenges us to see that:

- Much of our suffering comes not from life itself, but from our *attachment to outcomes.*
- Fate is not a force, but a label we slap on surprises.
- Real wisdom may lie in reducing assumptions—not trying to control outcomes.

This tale leaves us with a quietly powerful truth: *The fewer your assumptions, the less you need fate to explain your life.*

11

ROOF-TOP CHARITY

One day, Nasruddin was busy repairing the tiles on the roof of his house when he heard a knock at the door.

Peering over the edge, he called down, "What do you want?"

A man below shouted, "Come down! I cannot shout it from here!"

With a groan, Nasruddin slowly climbed down the ladder, wiping sweat from his brow.

"Well?" he asked. "What was so urgent?"

"I am just a poor old man," the stranger said, holding out his hand. "Could you spare a few coins?"

Without a word, Nasruddin turned and began climbing back up the ladder.

Puzzled but hopeful, the beggar followed him.

When they were both standing on the roof, Nasruddin turned to him and said calmly, "*The answer is no.*"

Commentary: The Irony of Effort and Expectation

This story is a classic example of Nasruddin's poetic justice wrapped in absurdity. At first glance, it seems petty—even cruel. But dig a little deeper, and you will see Nasruddin offering a masterclass in boundaries, absurdity, and proportionate effort.

The beggar:

- Disregards Nasruddin's labour and exhaustion.
- Demands attention without reason.
- Asks for something without even the courtesy of clarity.

And so, Nasruddin mirrors the situation perfectly: if the beggar made him come down *just to say something unnecessary*, then *he too shall go up for something unnecessary.*

The lesson?

- Don't make others work harder for your request than you've worked for your need.
- Respect people's time, energy, and current context.
- And above all: sometimes, a witty *"No"* can carry more teaching value than a hundred lectures.

It is Nasruddin at his finest—making you laugh first... and think later.

12

LOOKING WHERE THE LIGHT IS

One day, Mulla Nasruddin was down in the dark, cluttered basement of his house when he dropped his precious ring. After fumbling around in vain, he gave up and climbed out into the sunlight.

Soon after, a neighbour noticed Nasruddin crawling around on the street, peering carefully at the ground.

"Mulla, what are you looking for?" he asked.

"My ring," Nasruddin replied.

"Where did you lose it?"

"In the basement," said the Mulla.

The neighbour blinked. "Then why on earth are you looking for it out here?"

Nasruddin threw up his hands and said, "Don't be ridiculous! It is far too dark in the basement. How can I possibly find anything down there?"

Commentary: Illumination Isn't Always Insight

This is one of Nasruddin's most deceptively simple stories, and yet it holds a powerful metaphor for the way we often deal with our own problems.

We tend to *search for solutions where it's easiest to look*, not where the problem actually lies:

- We distract ourselves from inner confusion with outward busyness.
- We avoid uncomfortable introspection by clinging to visible, external fixes.

- We seek clarity in bright places—but the source of our struggle remains buried in shadow.

Nasruddin's behaviour is absurd—but only in the way that most of us behave when we're avoiding emotional or psychological darkness. Instead of dealing with the issue *where it actually exists* (in the basement), we go searching *where there is light* (on the street)—because it's more comfortable, more visible, more socially acceptable.

The moral?

Comfort is not clarity! Light does not guarantee truth! And sometimes, to find what you have truly lost, you must be willing to step into the dark.

13

RIGHT, RIGHT... AND ALSO RIGHT

One day, Judge Mulla Nasruddin was presiding over a dispute in court.

The plaintiff spoke first, passionately laying out his arguments. When he finished, Nasruddin nodded thoughtfully and said, "You are right!"

Then the defendant rose, delivering his version of the events with equal passion.

Nasruddin nodded again. "Yes, you are right!"

His wife, who had been quietly observing from the side, frowned and said, "That does not make any sense, Mulla. Both of them cannot be right!"

Nasruddin looked at her, smiled, and said, "You know what? You are right, too!"

Commentary: The Foolish Wisdom of Agreeing with Everyone

This story is a classic Nasruddin twist—hilarious on the surface, deceptively deep underneath.

At first glance, it appears that the Mulla is being absurd, agreeing with both sides—and then even with his wife who contradicts them. But beneath the comedy lies a subtle commentary on *the nature of truth, perception, and human diplomacy.*

It illustrates:

- How people *seek affirmation more than objectivity*.
- That in disputes, both parties often believe they are right—because *truth is subjective and emotionally tinted*.
- And that sometimes, *agreeing with everyone is less about logic and more about avoiding conflict*—a tool many use in relationships, politics, and even the courtroom.

Nasruddin's final line turns the whole exchange into a circle of irony, making us laugh—*not because it makes sense, but because it mirrors the way people often talk in real life.*

The lesson?

Not every judgment seeks justice—some just seek peace. And in the court of human behaviour, logic sometimes takes the day off.

14

THE ROYAL VEGETABLE

Mulla Nasruddin had become a regular presence at the royal court, known not just for his wit but also for cleverly exposing the absurdities of courtly behaviour.

One afternoon, the King, ravenous from a long hunt, was served a dish of perfectly cooked aubergines.

Delighted, he exclaimed, "These are divine! Chef, serve them every day!"

He turned to Nasruddin and asked, "Aren't aubergines the best vegetable in the world, Mulla?"

Nasruddin bowed. "The very best, Your Majesty."

And so, the palace was flooded with aubergine dishes—roasted, stewed, stuffed, and sliced. For breakfast, lunch, and dinner.

After the tenth meal in five days, the King slammed his spoon on the table. "Enough! Take these things away—I *hate* aubergines!"

Nasruddin, without missing a beat, nodded solemnly. "They are the worst vegetable in the world, Majesty."

The King blinked. "Mulla… just a few days ago, you called them the best!"

"I did," said Nasruddin. "But I am the servant of the King—not of the vegetable."

Commentary: Loyalty, Flattery, and Flexible Truth

This tale is classic Nasruddin: quick wit wrapped around an inconvenient truth.

At face value, it is a playful jab at *sycophants*—those who shift their loyalties and opinions with the winds of power. Nasruddin's honesty is paradoxical: he admits he is *not* loyal to the aubergine because his role is to reflect the will of the King.

But beneath the humour lies an astute observation of how power distorts truth:

- In the court of authority, *truth bends to favour*, not fact.
- *Flattery is currency*, and survival often depends on knowing when to praise and when to pivot.
- And sometimes, *saying what people want to hear* is the quickest path to keeping your head—and your job.

The brilliance of Nasruddin is that he doesn't flatter blindly. He flatters *consciously*, exposing the court's hypocrisy *by participating in it just enough to mirror it.*

The message?

In a world ruled by ego and appetite, those who speak the truth may not last long—unless, of course, they do it with a twinkle in their eye and a twist of the tongue.

15

THE ONE-EYED TIGERS

While visiting India, Mulla Nasruddin was told that no journey to the subcontinent would be complete without a tiger hunt.

"It is quite simple," his hosts explained. "Tie a bleating goat to a tree at dusk. When the tiger hears the cries, he'll come prowling. You climb a tree nearby, wait with your rifle, and when the tiger appears—aim straight between the eyes and fire!"

The next day, the curious townspeople gathered to hear of Mulla's grand adventure.

"Well?" they asked. "Did you bag a tiger?"

Nasruddin shook his head. "No luck at all."

"Why? What happened?"

"These Indian tigers," he sighed, "are far too clever. They travel in pairs… and each one closes one eye. So of course, I missed them every time!"

Commentary: The Precision of Misplaced Logic

This story is a delightful example of Nasruddin's unmatched ability to blend absurd logic with impeccable delivery.

At first glance, it is nothing more than a silly excuse for bad aim. But listen closely, and you will hear a subtle dig at those who explain their failures with overly elaborate reasoning, rather than admitting their own shortcomings.

Mulla doesn't say:

- He missed the shot.
- He was nervous.
- He never saw a tiger.

Instead, he invents a hilariously intricate theory: that tigers conspire in pairs and outwit hunters by winking.

The message?

- People often use logic not to understand the truth, but to protect their ego.
- Excuses can be intelligent-sounding—and still completely ridiculous.
- And perhaps most importantly: *just because something sounds clever, does not mean it is not completely made up*.

Nasruddin once again reminds us that the real joke is not always what is said—*it is who believes it, and why.*

16

A DOUBLE DOSE OF DOCTORS

Mulla Nasruddin was beginning to show the wear and tear of his fondness for drink. Concerned, his doctor gave him a stern warning.

"Mulla, you must cut out alcohol altogether."

"I cannot just *stop*, Doctor!" Nasruddin cried. "That would kill me!"

The doctor nodded sympathetically. "All right then, let's take it step by step. This week, limit yourself to four double scotches a day. No more. Next week, bring it down to three. Then two."

Nasruddin nodded solemnly and staggered out of the clinic.

A week later, he returned—*completely sloshed.*

The doctor was furious. "What on earth are you doing? I told you—just four doubles a day!"

"I *followed* your instructions, Doctor," Nasruddin slurred. "But after I left your office, I got a second opinion… *and he prescribed the same treatment*!"

Commentary: Confirmation Bias with a Twist of Lime

This tale is vintage Nasruddin: hilarious in its delivery and painfully relatable in its truth.

Rather than confront his habit, Mulla does what many do when faced with difficult instructions—*he shops around for advice until he hears what he wants*. In this case, he hears it *twice* and doubles his dose with a straight face.

There's brilliance in the absurdity:

- *We often confuse validation with wisdom.*
- *Second opinions can easily become excuses for indulgence.*
- And when we *want* to continue a habit, we'll *always* find a way to justify it—especially if it is bottled.

Mulla's punchline is a satirical reminder of how cleverly people rationalize what they already intend to do.

The moral?

You can get second opinions all day—but it will not change the fact that you are the one pouring the drink.

17

THE TURBAN OF KNOWLEDGE

One day, an illiterate villager came to Mulla Nasruddin, clutching a sealed letter.

"Mulla," he said, "please read this letter to me. I cannot read."

Nasruddin took the letter and squinted at it—but the script was illegible, perhaps written in a different language or simply too messy to decipher.

"I am sorry," Nasruddin said, handing it back, "I cannot read this either."

The man was outraged. "Shame on you, Mulla! You wear that *turban*—the sign of wisdom and education—and yet you cannot read a simple letter?"

Without missing a beat, Nasruddin calmly removed the turban from his own head and placed it on the man's.

"There," he said. "Now *you* wear the turban. If it gives knowledge, read the letter yourself."

Commentary: Symbols Don't Equal Substance

This classic tale is a brilliant satire on how society often confuses *symbols of wisdom* with wisdom itself.

The turban, in many cultures, is a symbol of scholarship, respect, or religious learning—but Nasruddin's quick wit reminds us: *Wearing the attire of a wise man does not make you wise.*

Through humour, the story exposes:

- The *misplaced reverence for appearances* over actual ability.
- The *folly of projecting blame* onto others for our own shortcomings.
- And the way people often *expect titles and symbols to carry the burden of knowledge.*

Nasruddin, instead of defending himself, uses role reversal to highlight the absurdity of the man's accusation—making his point without a single word of argument.

The lesson?

Wisdom isn't in the turban—it is in the mind. And just because someone wears the robes of learning does not mean they hold the lessons within.

18

ALEXANDER THE GREAT... MUSLIM PROPHET?

While on a pilgrimage to Mecca, Mulla Nasruddin passed through Medina. As he strolled past the grand mosque, a tourist—looking thoroughly lost—approached him.

"Excuse me, sir," the tourist said, "you look like a local. This mosque looks ancient and important, but I've lost my guidebook. Could you tell me something about it?"

Too proud to admit he had no clue himself, Nasruddin beamed with confident authority.

"Ah yes! This mosque is incredibly special. It was built by Alexander the Great to commemorate his conquest of Arabia."

The tourist blinked in admiration but then paused. "Wait… wasn't Alexander the Great Greek? Not Muslim?"

Nasruddin nodded solemnly. "True. But he was so grateful for his victories, he converted to Islam out of sheer devotion."

"But wasn't Islam founded much later?" the tourist asked.

"Brilliant observation!" Nasruddin said. "Alexander was so inspired that he actually *founded* Islam himself."

The tourist gasped. "But… I thought Islam was founded by a man named Mohammed?"

"Exactly," said Nasruddin. "Once Alexander gave up his old life, he took a new name—*Mohammed*—so he could start afresh as a prophet."

The tourist looked thoroughly stunned.

"But didn't Alexander live centuries before Mohammed?" he asked finally.

Nasruddin gave a patient smile. "Ah! You are confusing him with a *different* Alexander the Great. I am speaking of the one named *Mohammed*."

Commentary: When Confidence Outruns Truth

This tale is a masterful portrait of what happens when pride, improvisation, and ignorance collide—and yet somehow manage to walk away unscathed.

Mulla Nasruddin's outrageous explanations reveal:

- How *ego resists admitting ignorance*, even when honesty would be far simpler.
- The ease with which *uninformed people can be impressed by confident nonsense.*
- And how the human mind, when cornered, will *construct increasingly absurd explanations to maintain the illusion of credibility.*

In many ways, this is a humorous warning against:

- Bluffing with false authority
- Blind acceptance of charismatic storytelling
- And the dangers of letting appearance and confidence substitute for actual knowledge

Nasruddin doesn't merely lie—he does so *with flourish*, layering falsehood over falsehood until it becomes an ornate monument of nonsense.

The takeaway?

In a world full of know-it-all's, be wary of those who would rather invent a new history than admit they do not know the facts.

19

POETRY IN PUNISHMENT

One day, the village mayor, proud of his newfound literary flair, read a poem aloud to Mulla Nasruddin.

"Well?" he asked eagerly. "Did you like it?"

Nasruddin shrugged. "Not really. It wasn't very good."

Furious, the mayor had him thrown in jail for three days.

A week later, the mayor summoned Nasruddin again and read him yet another poem—this time with greater theatrical flourish.

As soon as the poem ended, Nasruddin stood up without a word and began heading for the door.

"Hey!" the mayor called out. "Where do you think you're going?"

"To jail," replied Nasruddin.

Commentary: The Price of Honesty—and the Humour in Knowing

This short tale packs a big punch with its dry wit and biting realism. At first glance, it's a joke about a tyrannical mayor and a smart-mouthed Nasruddin. But beneath the humour lies a rich commentary on:

- The *fragility of ego*, especially when cloaked in authority.
- The *punishment of honesty* in places where flattery is expected.
- And how Nasruddin, instead of resisting injustice with anger, meets it with absurd logic and disarming wit.

Rather than argue or lie, Nasruddin simply prepares himself for the inevitable. His pre-emptive trip to jail is both hilarious and brilliant—it exposes the mayor's vanity while letting Nasruddin keep his dignity *and* his honesty.

The lesson?

When truth is punished and flattery is rewarded, the wise prepare not for applause—but for prison.

20

ONE-WAY ATTENDANCE

One morning, Nasruddin's wife rushed into the room.

"Husband, get up and get dressed quickly! We are running late for the mayor's funeral!"

Nasruddin turned over in bed, yawned, and replied, "Why should I rush to his funeral? It is not like *he's* going to show up for *mine*."

Commentary: The Logic of Self-Interest with a Side of Sass

This story is classic Nasruddin—blending irreverence with a razor-sharp twist of logic.

At first, his reply seems callous, almost disrespectful. But look again—it's a sardonic comment on:

- *Empty formalities and social obligations* we fulfil out of expectation rather than meaning.
- *Self-serving reciprocity*, where our actions are measured not by empathy, but by what we get in return.
- And the human tendency to *prioritize convenience over ceremony*, especially when sentiment is absent.

Mulla's wit lies in flipping the unspoken rules of etiquette. Instead of paying respects out of tradition or morality, he asks: *What is the point, if the favour cannot be returned?*

The humour is dark—but the truth is sharp.

The lesson?

We often go through the motions for the dead… but it is the living who decide whether those gestures are genuine or just tradition in a tailored suit.

21

DESTINATION: DOUBT

Mulla Nasruddin stepped onto a subway car clearly marked *TIMES SQUARE* in multiple places. Taking a seat next to a large man engrossed in his newspaper, Nasruddin leaned over politely and asked, "Excuse me, sir… does this train go to Times Square?"

Without looking up, the man grunted, "Yes, it does."

Moments later, Nasruddin asked again, "Are you *sure* it goes to Times Square?"

Now irritated, the man replied sharply, "Of course, I am sure!"

"But how can you *really* be sure?" Nasruddin persisted.

That did it.

The man slapped his newspaper shut and barked, "Can't you read? It says *TIMES SQUARE* all over this car! What more do you need?"

Embarrassed, Nasruddin shrank back into silence.

At the next stop, a nervous passenger entered the car and approached Nasruddin, asking hesitantly, "Excuse me… does this train go to Times Square?"

Nasruddin jumped to his feet, threw up his hands, and snapped, "*Now look what you have done! You have made me uncertain again*!"

Commentary: The Fragility of Certainty

This laugh-out-loud tale is a perfect snapshot of human psychology—how easily *certainty gives way to doubt* when questioned, no matter how obvious the truth may be.

At its heart, the story plays with:

- The *suggestibility of the mind*, even in the face of clear facts.
- How confidence—*or the lack of it in others*—can plant seeds of insecurity.
- And the subtle humour in our craving for external validation, even when the truth is staring us in the face (or plastered all over the subway walls).

Nasruddin's final outburst is hilarious because it is so *relatable*—how often do we find ourselves rethinking what we were sure of, just because someone else questioned it?

The deeper insight?

Certainty is not always anchored in truth—it is often tethered to confidence. And even the obvious can become doubtful... when others look unsure.

22

COLD LOGIC, HOT REVENGE

On a bitterly cold winter day, Mulla Nasruddin sat in the village coffeehouse with his friends, sipping tea and discussing the weather.

"I could stay out all night in this cold without needing any heat," boasted Nasruddin.

His friends laughed. "Is that so? Then let us make it interesting. Stand all night in the village square—no fire, no blankets, no shelter. If you do, we will each treat you to a lavish meal. But if you fail, *you* feed all of us."

"Done," said Nasruddin confidently.

That very night, he stood in the snow-covered square till dawn—shivering but never seeking warmth.

In the morning, he triumphantly returned. "Prepare your stomachs, my friends. I've earned a feast!"

"Not so fast," said one of them. "I saw a candle burning in a window three hundred yards away. That counts as external warmth. You lose."

"No one could possibly warm themselves from such a distance!" protested Nasruddin.

But his friends held firm. A bet was a bet—and Nasruddin had, in their eyes, lost.

He accepted their verdict with a calm nod and invited them all to his house for dinner that evening.

When they arrived, their mouths watered with anticipation. But time passed, and no food was served.

Finally, they barged into the kitchen—only to find Nasruddin standing by a huge cooking pot suspended from the ceiling. Beneath it, barely flickering, was a single candle.

"What on earth is going on?" they cried. "How could you possibly cook anything like this?"

Nasruddin smiled. "Why not? If a candle 300 yards away can keep me warm, surely this one three inches below the pot can cook dinner, right?"

Commentary: When Logic Freezes Over

This story is a masterstroke of *ironic justice* and *philosophical wit.* With humour as his sword, Nasruddin skewers the hypocrisy and flawed reasoning of those who twist logic to serve their convenience.

The key insights:

- Logic without empathy becomes absurd.
- Fairness is not about rigid rules, but consistent principles.
- And most importantly, hypocrisy is best defeated not with anger—but with a spoonful of satire.

Nasruddin's response is not just humorous—it is *profoundly educational.* He does not argue his case; he *demonstrates* the absurdity of their claim by turning it back on them, like a true Socratic sage wrapped in a jester's robe.

The lesson?

When people use logic selectively, the best rebuttal isn't protest—it is parody.

23

BY ORDER OF MY WIFE

At Heaven's gates, Saint Peter was organizing the influx of newly arrived souls to streamline divine processing.

"Alright," he announced, "All men, step forward first. We will sort out the women later."

As the men lined up, Saint Peter continued, "Now, all married men—divide yourselves into two lines. One for those who were *boss* in the family. The other for those who were... shall we say... *managed* by their wives."

In a blink, the line of henpecked husbands stretched long and winding, filled with resigned shoulders and knowing glances.

The other line—for the self-declared household heads—remained completely empty.

Except for one man: *Mulla Nasruddin.*

Saint Peter raised an eyebrow and walked over. "You do know what this line is for, don't you? It is for men who were in charge in their marriage."

"Yes, sir," muttered Nasruddin quietly.

"And you are *sure* you belong here?"

"I have to be," said Nasruddin with a sigh. "*My wife insists!*"

Commentary: The Illusion of Authority

This gem is a beautiful example of Nasruddin's ability to mock serious institutions—like marriage, masculinity, and ego—with a single punch-line.

Behind the laughter lies a rich blend of insight:

- Many relationships are driven by the *illusion of control.*
- Even in moments meant to declare independence or strength, people often follow invisible scripts.
- And perhaps most humorously, those who appear *in charge* are sometimes just following orders—*more obedient than they would ever admit.*

Nasruddin, as always, plays the fool—but delivers the final laugh with masterful timing. By *obeying his wife's command to be the boss*, he flips the whole concept of leadership on its head.

The lesson?

Sometimes, the one who thinks he is leading… is just the one marching in front of a parade he did not plan.

24

THE UPWARD DIG OF DOWNWARD WIT

There was a rather eccentric gentlemen's club in town that met every Tuesday evening. One of their founding rules was simple: *Any man who asked a question in the clubroom that he could not answer himself would be fined ten gold coins.*

One such Tuesday, Mulla Nasruddin rose and asked,

"Why doesn't a ground squirrel leave any dirt around the top of its hole when it digs it?"

A thoughtful silence filled the room. After some murmurs and shrugged shoulders, the members admitted defeat.

"All right, Mulla," said the chairman, "you win. What is the answer?"

Nasruddin replied coolly, "That is easy. The squirrel starts at the bottom and digs up."

The crowd erupted in amused groans—until one sharp fellow challenged, "But wait—how does it get to the bottom to begin with?"

Without missing a beat, Nasruddin grinned and said, "That, my friend, is *your* question."

Commentary: Mind the Logic Trap

This story is a prime example of Nasruddin's trademark ability to twist logic just far enough to sound reasonable—while secretly tying it in knots.

It playfully touches on:

- The absurdity of *circular reasoning.*
- The human tendency to accept *illogical answers* when delivered with confidence.
- And the subtle art of *dodging responsibility* by flipping the burden of proof.

In the end, Nasruddin turns a silly riddle into a game of mental ping-pong—and wins not with facts, but with wit.

The real lesson?

When people argue with more cleverness than truth, the smartest move is knowing when to laugh and let it go.

25

DOUBLE TROUBLE, TWICE THE PRAYERS

One day, Hamdi, a deeply frustrated man, approached Mulla Nasruddin with weary eyes and a heart full of woe.

"Mulla," he sighed, "I don't know what to do anymore. My wife is constantly complaining. I am either too fast or too slow, too quiet or too loud, too distant or too clingy. Nothing I do seems right. She grumbles about everything!"

Nasruddin nodded sagely and said, "Ah, my dear Hamdi, there is but one solution. You must do what I did—*take a second wife.*"

Hamdi's eyes widened with hope. "So that when the first starts complaining…"

"…you can escape to the second!" Nasruddin finished with a knowing smile. "Peace, my friend, is all about balance."

Hamdi joyfully followed the advice. With help from a matchmaker, he found a second wife. For a short while, everything seemed perfect.

But soon, reality struck. Instead of one complaining voice, he now had two. When he left one, the other chased him away. There were days when even the comfort of his own bed was denied to him.

Exhausted and desperate, Hamdi began spending his nights sleeping on the cold floor of the mosque. There, in the silence of despair, he would whisper his miseries into the void.

One night, as he shuffled into the mosque, he was shocked to see Nasruddin already there, seated in quiet contemplation.

"You!" Hamdi snapped. "*You!* You are the reason my life has turned from one storm into two hurricanes! If I were just miserable with one wife, I could live with it. But now, thanks to your brilliant counsel, both have joined forces—and I have no place to sleep! Why in the world would you ever give me such advice?"

Nasruddin looked up calmly and said, "Well, my friend… I needed some company for my nightly prayers."

Commentary: Shared Misery Is Half the Joke

This tale hilariously exposes the age-old fallacy that *multiplying options solves our problems.* Nasruddin offers Hamdi a solution that appears to promise relief—but delivers an even bigger headache. Yet, instead of apologizing, the Mulla turns the blame into a moment of companionship and wit.

The takeaways are multilayered:

- Escaping discomfort does not guarantee comfort.
- Sometimes we leap into new chaos thinking it is a solution—only to discover it is the same problem, twice.
- And most cleverly, even wise men seek misery... if it gives them someone to laugh and pray with.

The wisdom?

Before you double your choices, make sure you are not doubling your consequences.

26

MADNESS, MAJESTICALLY MISUNDERSTOOD

Nasruddin was informed that the Sultan himself would be visiting the province—and he, as one of the region's notables, would be presented at court.

There was only one problem: Nasruddin had absolutely no idea how to behave in front of royalty.

A royal equerry pulled him aside just before the audience and quickly coached him. "The Sultan will likely ask you three things:

1. How long you've lived here,
2. How long you've studied to become a Mulla, and
3. Whether you are satisfied with the spiritual health and taxation of the people."

Nasruddin nodded and memorized his responses carefully.

Soon enough, he was brought before the Sultan.

The monarch looked at him and asked, "How long have you studied?"

"Thirty-five years," replied Nasruddin proudly.

The Sultan frowned. "How old are you, then?"

"Twelve," came the reply.

The Sultan blinked in disbelief. "That's impossible! Are you mad, man?"

Nasruddin looked at him thoughtfully. "Yes, Your Majesty. We *both* are."

The Sultan bristled. "You dare to call *me* mad?"

Nasruddin bowed slightly and said, "Indeed, Your Majesty. But we are mad in different ways!"

Commentary: When Logic Bows to Absurdity

This short tale skewers the blind reliance on memorized responses and the awkward absurdity that arises when order collapses. But underneath the surface-level humour lies deeper insight into:

- The fragility of appearances.
- The absurdity of rigid formality.
- And most tellingly, *the courage it takes to be honest*—even when the truth is laughable.

Nasruddin, cornered by his own confused sequence, does not try to untangle it—he embraces the absurdity, levelling the royal playing field with a cheeky "*we are all mad in our own way.*"

The deeper lesson?

Wisdom does not always speak in order—or wear a crown. Sometimes, it shows up in jumbled answers and an untamed sense of humour.

27

THE PURSUIT OF PERFECTION (AND WHY IT REMAINS UNMARRIED)

One evening at the teahouse, someone asked Nasruddin, "Tell us, Mulla—did you never want to get married?"

"Of course, I did," replied Nasruddin, stroking his beard thoughtfully. "In my youth, I was obsessed with finding the *perfect woman*."

He continued:

"First, I met a woman who was breathtakingly beautiful and deeply spiritual. But alas, she knew nothing of the world and its ways.

So, I kept searching and found another—wise in both heavenly matters and worldly affairs. But… she was terribly plain, and I feared I would go blind from trying to admire her.

Then finally, after years of searching far and wide, I met *her*—the one. She was beautiful, wise, practical, and spiritual. Everything I could ever dream of."

The listeners leaned in, holding their breath. "So? Why did you not marry her, Mulla?"

Nasruddin shrugged and sighed, "Well… *she* was looking for the perfect man."

Commentary: The Imperfection of Perfect Expectations

In true Nasruddin style, this story playfully reveals a profound truth about human nature: *the endless search for perfection often ends in lonely irony.*

We set out looking for flawless partners, employees, jobs, or friends—and forget that we, too, are part of the equation. The very standards we set may be the ones that keep us apart from happiness.

Those chasing perfection often forget that perfection may be busy chasing someone else—or does not exist at all.

Nasruddin's wit reminds us:

- Companionship thrives not in flawlessness, but in acceptance.
- The perfect is often the enemy of the good.
- And the real wisdom? Laugh at the chase and embrace the human dance of imperfections.

Because sometimes, the only thing more foolish than expecting perfection from others… is expecting it from ourselves.

28

THE FIERCE APPLICANT

Mulla Nasruddin once went to a factory to apply for the position of night security guard.

The manager sized him up, then frowned.

"Mr. Nasruddin," he began, "this is a serious position. We need someone who is tough, fearless, aggressive, suspicious, distrustful—always on edge, constantly ready to jump into action and confront trouble without hesitation."

He leaned in closer. "Frankly, you don't seem to fit the bill at all."

Nasruddin smiled calmly and replied, "Oh, that is quite all right. I am not applying for myself. I came on behalf of my wife."

Commentary: Be Careful What You're Qualified For

This story delivers a hilarious punchline with a hidden sting—revealing how some traits that are unpleasant in domestic life are often seen as valuable in certain professions.

Nasruddin's quip points out:

- How qualities like suspicion and aggression may be admired in some settings but disastrous in others (like marriage).
- How we often stereotype roles based on traits without considering context or consequences.

- And humorously, it flips the mirror toward domestic dynamics—where a fiery temper at home can turn someone into a *perfect* candidate… for security duty.

Wisdom does not always arrive with a straight face. Sometimes, it knocks on the door disguised as a job applicant—with a recommendation letter from home.

29

THE PRICE OF PARENTAL FAME

Mulla Nasruddin was beaming with pride as he met his neighbour on the street.

"Did you hear about my son?" he asked, puffing out his chest.

"No," replied the neighbour, "what about him?"

"He is going to a psychiatrist," Nasruddin said proudly. "Twice a week!"

The neighbour blinked. "Uh… is that something to be proud of?"

"Absolutely!" Nasruddin grinned. "He pays forty rupees an hour—and all he talks about is *me!*"

Commentary: Ego, Redefined

In true Nasruddin fashion, this story brilliantly flips conventional logic on its head. What might be seen as a concern by others—needing therapy—is transformed into a bizarre badge of honour.

Nasruddin's pride in being the subject of expensive therapy sessions highlights:

- Our *desire for relevance*—even if it's for the wrong reasons.
- The human tendency to *spin any situation into a win*, especially when ego is involved.
- The absurd lengths people go to, *to feel important*—even if it's because they caused the trauma.

Sometimes, the need to matter trumps the need to be right—or even kind. And in Nasruddin's world, if you are being talked about, you are already halfway to being famous.

This tale is a humorous reminder that self-awareness doesn't always come with a price tag—but delusion might.

30

THE TICKET THAT WASN'T

Mulla Nasruddin was pulled over by a patrolman for speeding.

As the officer prepared to write a ticket, a voice from the back seat erupted:

"There! I told you this would happen! You never listen. Speeding, cutting corners, ignoring stop signs, no horn, no brains—and now look! I told you so, didn't I? Didn't I?!"

The patrolman paused mid-pen and leaned toward the window.

"Who is that woman?" he asked.

Nasruddin sighed, "That is my wife."

The patrolman quietly put his ticket book away, looked Nasruddin in the eye, and said,

"Drive on. You have been punished enough."

Commentary: The Everyday Comedy of Life

This story offers one of those delightful moments where truth, comedy, and human nature collide in perfect absurdity.

Nasruddin, though clearly guilty of speeding, is instantly seen as a victim of a *greater sentence*: enduring relentless nagging. The patrolman's unexpected mercy reveals:

- How emotional penalties sometimes outweigh legal ones.
- That comedy often lies in recognition—*we have all been there*, on one side or the other.

- And most of all, how *human connection* (or commiseration) can soften even the arm of the law.

Sometimes justice is not found in a courtroom—but in the silent understanding between two men who have both lost arguments before they even started.

In classic Nasruddin fashion, we laugh—but also nod in knowing sympathy.

31

DEBT OF GRATITUDE (AND DAMPNESS)

One day, Mulla Nasruddin nearly slipped and fell into a pool.

A man nearby—someone Nasruddin barely knew—grabbed his arm just in time and saved him from an embarrassing plunge.

From that day on, the man never missed a chance to remind Nasruddin of his *heroic rescue*.

Every time they met, it was the same story. "You remember how I saved you? You could have drowned! You owe me your life!"

Eventually, Nasruddin had had enough.

He took the man back to the same pool, jumped in, and surfaced with his head just above water.

Then he shouted, "There! Now I am just as wet as I would have been if you had not saved me! Now let us call it even!"

Commentary: Freedom from the Chains of Gratitude

This story hilariously exposes the dark side of favours—when they're weaponized as emotional leverage.

While true gratitude is noble, Nasruddin reminds us of the importance of boundaries:

- A good deed done to serve the ego is not a gift *but a trap*.
- When *kindness turns into currency*, it loses its moral value.
- Gratitude is meaningful only when it flows freely—not when it is *extracted like a tax*.

Some people help you out of the water—then spend the rest of their lives trying to keep you drowning in obligation.

Once again, Nasruddin dives straight into the heart of human nature—and comes out dripping with wisdom.

32

TWICE THE WIFE, TWICE THE WOE

Hamdi was at his wit's end.

"Mullah," he complained, "I don't know what to do anymore! My wife grumbles all day—I am too slow, too fast, eat too much, eat too little, stay at home too often, go out too much, don't talk enough or talk too much! I am suffocating!"

Nasruddin nodded sympathetically. "Ah, there is only one way out of such hardship."

"Really?" asked Hamdi, eyes lighting up.

"Yes," said Nasruddin, "Go and get yourself a second wife—just like I did! That way, when your first wife starts complaining, you can escape to the second!"

Hamdi clapped his hands in glee. "Brilliant!"

Excited, he found a matchmaker and soon married again. For a brief while, life was peaceful.

But reality quickly caught up.

When Wife One scolded him, he fled to Wife Two—only to be chased out again. Soon, both wives were grumbling in stereo. He had no peace, no bed, and no refuge—except the mosque, where he began spending his nights in prayer and silent lament.

One cold evening, he stumbled in, frustrated and tired—only to find Nasruddin already there.

"*You*!" Hamdi shouted. "You are the reason I am doubly miserable! If it were not for your advice, I would still be happily unhappy with just one woman. Now two of them have turned my life into a living hell! Why did you do this to me?"

Nasruddin looked up serenely and smiled, "Well, to be honest, I was lonely. I just wanted some company for my nightly prayers."

Commentary: Solutions That Backfire

This tale is a brilliant satire on how *quick-fix solutions often create double the trouble*. Instead of addressing his core problem—communication and emotional mismatch—Hamdi tries to escape it by multiplying the very source of his misery.

Through Nasruddin's comical manipulation, we uncover deeper truths:

- You cannot *solve internal conflicts with external additions*.
- Trying to outrun your problems might just give them *more legs*.
- And most hilariously, advice—even when well-intentioned—is often more about *the advisor's needs than the recipient's*.

Doubling your options doesn't always double your joy—sometimes it just doubles your headaches.

As always, Nasruddin's mischief leads to a moral, and his mischief-maker's wisdom shines through the absurdity.

33

MISTAKEN FOR GOD (REPEATEDLY)

Mulla Nasruddin was enjoying an afternoon at the teahouse with two of his friends, all of them puffed up with self-importance, talking about how their faces bore striking resemblances to famous people.

The first man said proudly, “Everywhere I go, people stare at me. They say I look exactly like Winston Churchill. A few even asked me to pose with cigars.”

The second chimed in, “That is nothing. People think I am President Nixon. I have even signed autographs ‘just to be polite’.”

Mulla Nasruddin remained silent for a moment, sipping his tea, then said with a shrug, “You both are amateurs.”

“What do you mean?” they asked.

“Well,” said Mulla Nasruddin, “*I* have been mistaken for God Himself!”

His two friends stared at him in disbelief. “God?! How?”

Nasruddin leaned back, put down his teacup, and with a perfectly serious face said, “When I was convicted and sent to jail for the *fourth* time, the jailer saw me, slapped his forehead, and exclaimed— ‘*OH GOD, YOU HAVE COME AGAIN!*’”

Commentary: Divine Recognition or Devilish Reputation?

This classic Nasruddin story is a masterpiece of comic timing and self-deprecating wit. On the surface, it appears as an absurd boast but look closer and you'll find layered insight.

- Nasruddin *twists the idea of fame*—while others compare themselves to global leaders with pride, he compares himself to the divine... but in the most ironically inglorious of settings: a jail cell.
- His *godly* recognition is not admiration—it is *exasperation*. And that is the brilliance of it.
- The punchline dismantles ego with humour—reminding us that *reputation isn't always equal to respect*. Sometimes, it is just predictable bad behaviour.

True enlightenment is when you can laugh at your own infamy—and still make others laugh too.

This story, like many of Nasruddin's, flips vanity into humility, and humility into humour. A divine joke, indeed!

34

CHICKEN SOUP FOR THE DEPARTED

During a popular theatre performance, the curtain suddenly dropped mid-act. A hushed confusion fell over the audience. Moments later, the theatre manager emerged, visibly shaken.

"Ladies and gentlemen," he said, "I regret to inform you that the great Mendel Kalb has just suffered a fatal heart attack backstage. The performance cannot continue."

From the balcony, a familiar voice rang out—Mulla Nasruddin, ever the unlikely source of solutions.

"Quick!" he shouted, "Give him some chicken soup!"

The manager, startled, tried to clarify, "Sir, the man is dead! Mendel Kalb has *passed away*!"

Nasruddin, undeterred, shouted again, "Then hurry up and give him some chicken soup!"

At this point, the exasperated manager cried out, "But sir, he is *dead*! What on earth will chicken soup do?"

Nasruddin stood tall, shrugged, and responded with divine simplicity: *"What harm?"*

Commentary: Hope, Humour, and the Human Condition

This story is Mulla Nasruddin at his paradoxical best—*irreverent yet wise, ridiculous yet profound.*

On the surface, it *is* hilariously absurd. Why would anyone recommend chicken soup for the dead? But that is precisely the brilliance of the tale.

- *Chicken soup* in many cultures is symbolic—not just of nourishment, but of comfort, healing, and maternal care. By suggesting it for the deceased, Nasruddin pokes fun at the human tendency to reach for familiar remedies in unfamiliar crises.
- More subtly, Nasruddin's logic ("What harm?") is a reminder that *sometimes our solutions may not be practical—but our intentions still reflect compassion.*
- He also exposes how people often react to tragedy: with helplessness, resignation, and silence. Mulla, instead, acts—albeit in his own oddball way.

There is something sacred about offering help—even when it seems too late. Especially when it seems too late.

This tale reminds us that *hope, even in futility, is still hope.* And sometimes, the last laugh carries the deepest truth.

35

NO PAIN, ALL GAIN—JUST NOT FOR HER

Mulla Nasruddin walked into the town dentist's clinic, his mind set on business—and bargains.

"I would like to know the cost of a tooth extraction," he asked.

"That will be four dollars," replied the dentist, "but if you would like it done painlessly, we'll need to administer gas—an additional three dollars."

Nasruddin quickly waved off the suggestion. "Forget the gas—we can save that three dollars."

The dentist, surprised and slightly impressed, said, "Well, you mountain folk are certainly tough. I must say, that is very brave of you."

Nasruddin nodded with a calm smile and replied:

"Oh, it is not me who's having the tooth pulled—it is my wife."

Commentary: When Frugality Gets Personal

This classic tale drips with Mulla Nasruddin's signature wit—and a pinch of *spousal insensitivity*!

On one level, it's a laugh-out-loud punchline about misplaced thrift. But underneath, it reveals some deeper human patterns:

- *Selective courage*: Nasruddin is only brave when it's someone else's pain.
- *Skewed empathy*: Saving a few coins sometimes takes precedence over someone else's suffering—especially if that someone is family.

- *Deadpan humour:* The real genius lies in the timing. Nasruddin lets the dentist—and the audience—believe he is the brave one, before flipping the narrative with perfect comedic precision.

The story is a cheeky reminder that *true compassion means more than just counting coins—it's about feeling for others as we do for ourselves.* And that, unfortunately, is where many fall short.

This parable tickles the funny bone while quietly tapping on the conscience.

36

THE MOON RESCUER OF RAMADAN

One calm night, as Nasruddin strolled past a well, an impulse made him glance into its depths. Gazing down, he was startled to see the reflection of the full Moon shimmering in the water.

His eyes widened. "Oh no! The poor Moon has fallen in," he gasped. "If I don't rescue her, she may never rise again—and Ramadan will never end!"

With noble urgency, he grabbed a rope, lowered it into the well, and shouted,

"Hold on tight! Help is on the way!"

The rope snagged on a rock, and Nasruddin, imagining he was pulling the Moon herself out of the water, tugged with all his might. Suddenly, the rope gave way, and Nasruddin tumbled backwards onto the ground.

He lay there catching his breath. Above him, the Moon sailed gracefully across the sky.

With a satisfied nod, Nasruddin smiled and said, "Well, that was close. Just as well I came by when I did!"

Commentary: A Reflection on Reflections

This whimsical tale is classic Nasruddin—foolish on the surface, but reflective (*pun intended*) of something profound.

On one hand, it is hilarious: a man tries to rescue the Moon's reflection from a well, convinced of his cosmic heroism.

But look deeper, and you find several layers of insight:

- *Mistaking appearance for reality*: The Moon wasn't trapped; only her image was. How often do we respond emotionally to reflections—of situations, people, or fears—without pausing to assess what's real?
- *Illusions of control*: Nasruddin's belief that the Moon (and by extension, the calendar of Ramadan) depends on *his* actions pokes fun at our over-inflated sense of agency in matters far beyond our control.
- *The need to feel helpful*: Even when nothing required fixing, Nasruddin assigns himself a saviour's role. The human ego is wired to seek purpose—even if it means inventing problems to solve.

As always, Mulla Nasruddin reminds us that humour is the mirror where wisdom often hides in plain sight.

37

THE BLAME GAME AND THE MISSING THIEVES

One day, Mulla Nasruddin and his wife returned home only to be greeted by a chilling sight—everything of value had vanished. The house had been burgled, top to bottom.

Immediately, his wife exploded in frustration: "This is all *your* fault! *You* should have locked the house properly!"

As if on cue, the neighbours gathered—and so did their judgments.

"You did not shut the windows!" cried one. "You should have known this would happen," said another.

"You knew the locks were old and still did not replace them," scolded a third.

Surrounded by finger-pointing voices, Nasruddin finally raised his hand and said calmly:

"Wait a moment—surely I am not the only one to blame here?"

"Well, who else could we blame?" they demanded.

Nasruddin shrugged. "What about the thieves?"

Commentary: When Accountability Becomes Absurd

This short tale masterfully illustrates how human nature leans toward blame—but often in the wrong direction.

Everyone's quick to pin fault on the victim or the one closest, while *the real culprit—the thief—is completely forgotten*. Nasruddin's remark, while comedic, is a sober reminder that:

- *Accountability is important, but context matters.* Blaming the one robbed more than the one robbing is not just unhelpful—it's absurd.
- *Hindsight bias runs rampant.* After an incident, it's easy to say what should've been done. But wisdom lies in preventing future mistakes, not flogging the past.
- *Victim-blaming is an ancient, persistent flaw.* Nasruddin's neighbours represent a society often too ready to criticize rather than empathize.

In his classic, deadpan style, Nasruddin teaches us: *Sometimes, common sense is the most uncommon thing in the crowd.*

38

SWEET DEAL, SALTY TWIST

One hot afternoon, Mulla Nasruddin and his friend stopped at a café, parched and panting. They ordered a single glass of milk and decided to share it.

"You drink your half first," said Nasruddin's friend, "because I have got just a pinch of sugar—enough for only one. I'll add it to *my* half."

"Why not add it now," suggested Nasruddin, "and I will drink only my half—sweet or not."

"Absolutely not," insisted the friend. "There is only enough sugar to sweeten *half* a glass, not the whole."

Nasruddin nodded calmly, walked up to the café owner, and returned with a large packet of salt.

"Good news, friend," he said cheerfully, "since I am drinking first, I would like my milk with salt."

Commentary: Tit for Tat in a Glass of Milk

This story serves up a deliciously clever lesson in fairness, reciprocity, and the art of not being taken for a fool.

Nasruddin's friend tries to game the system—sweetening *his* share while denying Nasruddin even the *chance* to decide. But Nasruddin flips the script with a salty twist.

Here's the deeper insight:

- *True sharing is about equality*; not selfish negotiation masked as logic.
- When one tries to *maximize gain at the other's expense*, they often invite a proportionate response.
- Nasruddin doesn't argue—he simply restores balance with quiet wit. It is not revenge; it is a recalibration.

Sometimes, the best way to expose selfishness is not through sermons—but through salted milk.

39

THE ENLIGHTENED FISH

On his long and winding quest for wisdom, Mulla Nasruddin passed a forest hut where a yogi sat deep in meditation. When the Master opened his eyes, Nasruddin bowed respectfully and asked, "Master, may I ask what you seek in such deep stillness?"

"I study every living creature," said the yogi, "in hopes that one day I might understand their language and commune with all animals."

"Well, then," said Nasruddin, "you would love to hear this—a fish once saved my life!"

The yogi, stunned, fell to his knees. "You holy man! Will you stay and teach me the path to such divine communion?"

Nasruddin agreed—on one condition: "First, Master, you must share all your knowledge with me. In turn, I will reveal my secret to you."

Three years passed. The yogi taught Nasruddin everything: about the habits of birds, the gestures of goats, the grammar of geckos. Finally, one morning, the yogi declared,

"I have fulfilled my part. It is time you teach me the language of the fish that saved you."

Nasruddin looked grave. "Are you sure you are ready? The truth may overwhelm you."

"I am ready!"

"Very well," said Nasruddin solemnly. "I was starving for nearly two months and close to death… when I finally caught a fish and ate it. It sustained me for three days."

Commentary: The Fish, the Fool, and the Finder of Meaning

This tale is a glorious skewering of *overcomplication in the pursuit of enlightenment.*

The yogi's quest—to *communicate with animals*—may be noble, but it blinds him to the obvious, practical, and lived wisdom that Nasruddin embodies. Where the yogi seeks metaphysical communion, Nasruddin simply *catches dinner* and survives.

The underlying lesson?

Many search for symbolic meaning when the truth is often refreshingly literal.

The joke is on us if we assume depth only lies in the mystical. Sometimes wisdom wears no robe, and enlightenment arrives on a plate, grilled with lemon.

40

THE SPIRIT AND THE FLESH

It was a lively party—wine, whisky, wit and whispers were flowing like a river in spring. Amidst this joyous tide stood a solemn, stiff-collared man—clearly a clergyman—wearing the expression of someone who'd been force-fed a lemon during baptism.

A waiter floated by with a tray of drinks.

"No, thank you," said the clergyman, pursing his lips. "I do not drink."

A few minutes later, another waiter—perhaps less briefed on theological preferences—offered him a fresh tray.

"I told you already," snapped the holy man, "I *never* drink alcohol. I would rather commit adultery than take a sip!"

At this, Mulla Nasruddin, quietly enjoying his whisky next door, suddenly stood up, set down his glass, and exclaimed with delight:

"GOOD HEAVENS! I HAD NO IDEA THERE WAS A CHOICE!"

Commentary: Morality on the Rocks

What seems like a cheap punchline at first reveals a deeper crack in the moral façade. The clergyman's hierarchy of sins is skewed—he demonizes one act while casually placing another (far more serious) sin as the lesser evil.

Nasruddin, ever the sharp observer, does not argue, moralize, or scold. He simply pokes fun at the absurdity of such rigid righteousness.

The deeper lesson?

When morality becomes performative, absurdity is inevitable.

By placing artificial restrictions above human realities, we sometimes forget that *true virtue is measured by compassion, not by abstinence.*

Also, Mulla reminds us: in a world full of choices, *know what you're choosing—and why.*

41

THE HONEST PROFESSION

Three young women and Mulla Nasruddin stood before the judge, a stern man who had clearly misplaced his sense of humour somewhere in the 1940s.

The women had been arrested for soliciting; Nasruddin, for peddling without a license.

The judge turned to the first girl. "What do you do for a living?"

"I am a fashion model, Your Honor."

"Thirty days," he barked.

Then to the second. "And you?"

"I am a television actress."

"Thirty days."

Then the third.

"I will be honest, Your Honor—I am a prostitute."

The judge adjusted his spectacles, nodded approvingly, and said, "For telling the truth, I will suspend your sentence."

Then he turned to Nasruddin.

"And you, sir, what is your occupation?"

Mulla twirled his hat, looked sincerely at the judge and said:

"To tell you the truth, Your Honor—I'm a prostitute too."

Commentary: Truth, Lies, and Tact

This story brilliantly lampoons how society and authority often reward *performative honesty* over actual integrity. Nasruddin, ever the opportunist with a philosopher's grin, spots a loophole in the logic—and dives in with a smirk.

Is he lying? Or simply pointing out that everyone, in some way, is selling *something*?

The deeper satire?

When truth becomes transactional, it ceases to be sacred.

Nasruddin's mock confession is both protest and performance—reminding us that in a world where honesty is inconsistently rewarded, irony becomes the sharpest form of truth.

42

THE QUESTION OF QUESTIONS

The prosecutor rose to cross-examine the witness—Mulla Nasruddin.

"Do you know this man?"

"How should I know him?"

"Did he borrow money from you?"

"Why should he borrow money from me?"

At this point, the judge—clearly losing patience—interjected sternly.

"Mulla, why do you persist in answering every question with another question?"

Mulla shrugged, raised an eyebrow and replied:

"Why not?"

Commentary: The Courtroom Philosopher

Mulla Nasruddin isn't just deflecting here—he is exposing the absurdity of forced logic. In a setting where answers are expected to be black or white, he tosses in the unpredictable shade of gray.

Where others see interrogation, Nasruddin sees *conversation*—and why should conversations be one-sided?

The Mulla's defence is not a legal strategy, it's a *philosophical judo throw.*

As the old saying goes:

"If you don't like the question, ask a better one in return."

43

THE PREVENTIVE STRIKE

Mulla Nasruddin handed a small boy a pot and sent him to fetch water from the well.

"Be careful," he warned. "Don't you dare break the pot!"

And just as the child turned to leave, *THWACK!* —Nasruddin gave him a swift slap across the head.

A stunned onlooker protested, "Mulla! Why would you hit the boy before he has even done anything wrong?"

Nasruddin replied, "You fool! What good is punishment *after* the damage is done?"

Commentary: The Insurance Policy of Blame

Nasruddin's logic may seem outrageous, but it slyly mirrors a very real human tendency—to worry in advance, to control the future, and sometimes, to punish people for things they *might* do, not for what they *did.*

This tale isn't just a humorous exaggeration; it is a mirror held up to our instinct for *pre-judgment and misplaced discipline.*

The Mulla's blow lands before the mistake does—but the story hits us *after* with a deeper meaning.

As the Persian proverb says:

"He who fears the future often punishes the present."

44

DEBTS OF HONOUR... OR OTHERWISE

"Brother," said Mulla Nasruddin to his neighbour, "I am collecting to help a poor man pay off a debt he cannot settle."

"How noble of you," said the neighbour, handing him a coin. "Who is this man?"

"Me," replied Nasruddin, and off he went.

Weeks later, he returned to the same door.

"I suppose you're here about a debt again?" said the now suspicious neighbour.

"I am," said Nasruddin.

"And I suppose someone can't pay up, and you want a contribution?"

"Correct again."

"I suppose it is you who owe the money?"

"Not this time."

"Well, that is a relief," the neighbour said, handing him another coin. "Now tell me, Mulla, what makes you so moved by the plight of this poor debtor?"

"Simple," said Nasruddin, tucking the coin away. "This time, *I am the creditor*!"

Commentary: A Man of Principles—Profitable Ones

Nasruddin's *generosity* is, once again, delightfully self-serving. Whether *as debtor or creditor*, the Mulla knows how to keep the cash flowing—always toward his own pockets.

Yet, the tale carries a subtle jab at how we disguise personal gain as public service. Charity is noble, yes—but sometimes, the person holding the collection bowl is also holding the IOU.

As they say in business:

"Never miss a chance to do well while doing good."

45

LET THE BOY LEARN

One evening at dusk, Mulla Nasruddin and his wife were sitting quietly on a park bench. On the other side of the hedge, unaware of their presence, a young man and his sweetheart took a seat.

Within moments, the young man began to whisper sweet nothings—his words dripping with affection, promises, and poetic declarations of eternal love.

Hearing this, Nasruddin's wife leaned over and whispered, "He doesn't know we are here. It sounds like he is about to propose. Mulla, shouldn't you cough or make a sound to warn him?"

"Why should I warn him?" Nasruddin replied dryly. "*Nobody warned me.*"

Commentary: No Spoilers, Please

This short and sharp story perfectly captures Mulla Nasruddin's eternal blend of mischievous wisdom and lived experience. There is no bitterness—only bemusement.

In his one-line refusal, Mulla says what many think but few dare to admit: some lessons must be lived, not learned second-hand.

As a modern twist might put it:

"If wisdom were contagious, love wouldn't still be making fools."

46

THE HAT AND THE HUMILITY

One fine afternoon, Mulla Nasruddin was walking proudly down the street, donning a brand-new hat. Just then, the sky turned grey, and it began to pour.

Not wanting his prized possession to get ruined, Nasruddin did what no one expected: he hiked up his robes and covered his head with them, shielding only the hat. His legs, waist-down, were completely exposed.

People on the street stared in disbelief, but Mulla walked on unbothered.

Finally, a well-meaning passerby couldn't resist and tapped him on the shoulder, saying,

"Mulla, I hate to point it out, but your... anatomy is rather embarrassingly uncovered!"

Nasruddin, cool as ever, replied, *"Well, sir, don't you realise my hat is new... but my anatomy is old?"*

Commentary: Age Before Modesty

This tale is Nasruddin logic at its finest—turning societal norms upside down with effortless justification. What others consider shameful, Mulla treats as practical. The story is not merely about vanity, but about how we assign value—often disproportionately—to things shiny and new, even at the cost of dignity.

As a humorous proverb might go:

"Better bare bones than a battered brim!"

47

A FREE HAND — BUT WHERE?

Mulla Nasruddin sat quietly, listening to his wife read aloud from the latest book on child psychology. Their son, known across the neighbourhood for his explosive tantrums and general chaos, had just broken a flowerpot and was now chasing a chicken indoors.

With great excitement, his wife read: *"It says here that we must give the child a completely free hand!"*

Mulla grunted, narrowed his eyes at the running menace, and replied with calm sarcasm:

"Does it indeed? And does it say where?"

Commentary: Books and Brats

Somewhere between parental theory and the war zone that is real parenting lies the wisdom of Nasruddin. He sees the absurdity of giving unchecked liberty to a child who already treats every object as either a weapon or a toy.

This story is not a dismissal of modern parenting, but a humorous reminder: *freedom without guidance is not parenting—it is surrender.*

As Mulla might say:

"Let the child run wild—but don't complain when he builds his kingdom on your head."

48

THE PILL THAT FIXED THE WRONG DAY

Mulla Nasruddin had been late to work one too many times. One morning, the boss snapped: "If you're late again, you're fired!"

Determined to fix the problem, Nasruddin visited a doctor who prescribed him a sleeping pill.

"Take this tonight," said the doctor, "and you will sleep soundly and wake up refreshed."

That night, Nasruddin took the pill, slept deeply, and woke up even before his alarm clock. He got dressed leisurely, enjoyed a hearty breakfast, and strolled into the office a full thirty minutes before anyone else.

When the boss walked in, Nasruddin greeted him proudly: "Well, I didn't have *any* trouble getting up this morning!"

The boss looked at him, dumbfounded. *"That's good, Mulla... but—WHERE WERE YOU YESTERDAY?"*

Commentary: Right Solution, Wrong Day

In classic Nasruddin fashion, he *does* solve the problem—but a day too late. This tale is a light-hearted jab at those of us who get the *method* right but miss the *moment.*

As Mulla might say:

"I was early for the wrong day—but on time for the lesson!"

49

THE FAST HORSE AND THE WET RIDER

A wealthy man once invited Mulla Nasruddin to join him on a hunting expedition. But while he mounted himself on a fine steed, he offered Nasruddin a slow, lumbering horse.

Nasruddin said nothing.

Soon, the hunt surged ahead, leaving the Mulla far behind. As fate would have it, dark clouds gathered, and a torrential downpour began. The rest of the party, in their haste, were drenched before they could reach shelter.

Nasruddin, on the other hand, quietly dismounted, folded his clothes neatly, and sat on them under the open sky. When the rain stopped, he dressed himself and returned — completely dry.

Back at the host's home, the soaked and shivering hunters were bewildered.

"How is it," they asked, "that you, with the slowest horse, remained dry?"

"Simple," replied Nasruddin, "It was the horse you gave me."

Intrigued, the next day the host offered Nasruddin the fastest horse and took the slow one himself. Again, it rained. Again, the host got soaked trying to gallop his way home. And again, Nasruddin used the same method — undressing, folding, sitting — and returned dry as ever.

This time, the host exploded:

"It is your fault! You made me take that wretched horse!"

"Perhaps," said Mulla Nasruddin gently, "you forgot to contribute anything of *your own* to the problem of keeping dry?"

Commentary: Blaming the Horse Doesn't Keep You Dry

Nasruddin reminds us that while external circumstances may be unfair, our response to them is entirely our own. Wisdom isn't always about speed — it's about sensibility.

As the Mulla might say:

"Blame the horse all you want, but it is *your* trousers that are dripping."

50

THANK YOU FOR NOT TREATING ME

One day, Mulla Nasruddin fell gravely ill. His worried wife, fearing the worst, rushed to the local doctor.

"Doctor," she pleaded, "my husband is seriously unwell. We are poor and have many children. If anything happens to him, who will care for us?"

The doctor, upon hearing the word *poor*, raised an eyebrow.

"Madam," he scoffed, "why burden the poor fellow even more? If you cannot afford the medicine, what is the point of me prescribing it?"

Disappointed, she returned home and told the Mulla what had happened.

A few days later, to everyone's surprise, Nasruddin made a full recovery. Once back on his feet, he walked straight to the doctor's clinic.

"Doctor," he said politely, "I just came to say thank you."

"Thank me?" said the doctor, confused. "But I didn't treat you!"

"Exactly!" Nasruddin grinned. "Had your foul breath come anywhere near me, who knows which cemetery I'd be fertilizing right now?"

Commentary: Sometimes the Cure Is Worse Than the Disease

The Mulla delivers a biting thank-you — quite literally. In this tale, he highlights the irony of self-important professionals who believe their mere presence is a blessing. Sometimes, as Nasruddin implies, *not helping is the best help you can give.*

"Some doctors save lives with medicine. Others, with absence."

51

I TRUSTED HIM

Mulla Nasruddin and his wife were on holiday in Israel. One evening, they decided to check out a popular nightclub in Tel Aviv. The headline act was a stand-up comedian performing entirely in Hebrew.

Throughout the show, Nasruddin's wife sat silently, puzzled by the language. But the Mulla? He roared with laughter at the end of each joke, slapping his knee and chuckling heartily.

Finally, when the comedian left the stage, she turned to him and said, "I didn't know you understood Hebrew!"

"I don't," Nasruddin replied cheerfully.

"Then why were you laughing so much?"

"Ah," said the Mulla, "I trusted him."

Commentary: The Leap of Faith Called Laughter

In a world where everyone tries to appear wise by understanding everything, Mulla Nasruddin reminds us that *sometimes you don't need to understand the language—just the joy.* His blind trust in the comedian reflects a unique kind of wisdom: not everything needs analysis to be enjoyed.

"True humour doesn't need translation—it just needs trust."

52

EGGISTENTIAL CRISIS

Mulla Nasruddin, looking unusually troubled, was consulting a psychiatrist.

"My wife," said the Mulla, "is convinced she is a chicken. She clucks and squawks all day long and sleeps on a wooden bar she is nailed to the wall like a perch."

The psychiatrist raised an eyebrow. "How long has this been going on?"

"Nearly two years."

The psychiatrist looked shocked. "Two years? Then why are you coming to me only now?"

Nasruddin blushed. "Well… to be honest… it was kind of nice having a steady supply of eggs."

Commentary: Cracked but Comfortable

Sometimes, we tolerate madness when it is convenient. Mulla Nasruddin's tale isn't just funny—it is a mirror to our own habits. We often let absurdities persist in our lives simply because they serve a purpose, however minor or irrational.

"Every madness feeds someone's comfort — until it doesn't."

53

THE SUICIDE SURVIVAL KIT

Mulla Nasruddin had been pulled from the river after what the police suspected was a suicide attempt. At headquarters, soaked and shivering, he admitted it.

"Yes, I tried to kill myself," said the Mulla. "The world has always been against me, so I decided to end it properly — no half-measures!"

"So, I bought a rope, a bottle of kerosene, a box of matches, and a loaded pistol. Just to be sure, I chose a tree by the river. I threw the rope over a branch, tied it around my neck, poured kerosene all over myself, struck a match to set myself on fire, then jumped into the river with the pistol to my head and pulled the trigger!"

The officer stared in disbelief. "And then what happened?"

"Wouldn't you know it?" said Nasruddin. "The bullet missed me and snapped the rope. I fell straight into the river, which put out the flames."

He paused and sighed, shaking his head. "And if I had not been such a good swimmer, I would have drowned myself!"

Commentary: When Nothing Goes According to Plan... Thankfully!

This parable is a darkly humorous reminder that even when we orchestrate disaster with careful precision, life has a way of botching our worst intentions. It is absurd, yes — but also profound. The very mishaps Mulla sees as failures may have been his salvation.

"Even doom has its loopholes — if you can swim."

54

THE BRAYING TRUTH

One day, Nasruddin's neighbour dropped by.

"Mulla, could I borrow your donkey?"

"Alas, I have already lent it out," replied Nasruddin solemnly.

Just then, from the stable behind the house, the unmistakable sound of a donkey braying echoed loudly.

"But Mulla!" exclaimed the neighbour, pointing, "I can *hear* the donkey right now!"

Without flinching, Nasruddin gently began closing the door and said with regal calm:

"My dear fellow, if you choose to trust the word of a donkey over that of a Mulla, then you are certainly not worthy of borrowing either."

And with that, the door clicked shut.

Commentary: The Donkey Dilemma – Truth, Lies, and Dignity

This classic tale of quick wit and quicker denial is vintage Nasruddin. Faced with being caught in a lie, he does not back down—instead, he elevates the act of fibbing into a lesson in misplaced trust.

In the age-old tug-of-war between truth and convenience, Nasruddin reminds us that *when facts are inconvenient, it is not about being right—it is about sounding righteous.*

"If truth knocks, shut the door. If dignity speaks, let it lie… especially if it's braying."

55

THE CASE OF THE VANISHING MEAT

One day, Mulla Nasruddin bought three *okes* (that is nearly 8.5 pounds) of meat and proudly brought it home for supper.

Later that evening, when he returned from work, he was surprised to find nothing but bread and onions on the table.

"Where's the meat?" he asked.

His wife looked distressed. "I rinsed it and set it aside, but that wretched cat snatched it and ran off!"

Nasruddin said nothing. Calmly, he fetched the kitchen scale, caught the cat, and weighed it.

Three *okes*. Exactly!

He turned to his wife with a raised eyebrow.

"Now listen carefully," he said, "if this here is the cat—then where is the meat? But if this is the meat—then where is the cat?"

Commentary: Scales of Justice and Domestic Mysteries

This is one of Nasruddin's most famous logical one-liners, showcasing his impeccable wit and razor-sharp deductive reasoning. It is less about catching his wife red-handed, and more about *exposing absurdity through absurd logic*.

In typical Nasruddin fashion, *he doesn't accuse—he measures*. And in doing so, he reveals more than the missing dinner: he unmasks the all-too-human instinct to lie poorly and cover up worse.

"When caught without proof, bring a scale. The truth weighs what words cannot."

56

THE BLESSING THAT BACKFIRED

Mulla Nasruddin and the village priest had long been at each other's throats. Their endless bickering finally brought them before the magistrate.

After hearing both sides, the weary magistrate sighed and said, "Surely, gentlemen, this can be resolved without further dispute. Shake hands and say something kind to each other."

The priest dutifully extended his hand, grasped Nasruddin's, and said with serene piety,

"I wish for you what you wish for me."

Nasruddin yanked his hand back and exclaimed, "See, Your Honour? He is starting again!"

Commentary: Mirror, Mirror, on the Mind

This short tale is a masterclass in *passive aggression* wrapped in religious politeness. The priest, cloaked in civility, offers what sounds like a blessing—but Nasruddin knows better. When intentions are murky, even kindness can carry a hidden sting.

Nasruddin's brilliance lies in how he unmasks the *subtle venom behind saccharine words.* His retort—simultaneously comic and cutting—reveals how true reconciliation needs more than formal gestures; it needs sincerity.

"Even sugar-coated curses taste bitter to those who know the cook."

57

THE CAKEWALK OF PERFECTIONISM

Mulla Nasruddin walked into a bakery and announced, "I want a birthday cake baked in the shape of the letter N."

The baker nodded and promised it would be ready by 2 p.m. "But it will cost you."

"Money is no object," declared the Mulla.

At two o'clock, the Mulla returned. The cake was presented. Nasruddin exploded:

"Not an ordinary N, you idiot! I wanted a beautiful flowing N in script!" The baker sighed but promised a new cake by 8 p.m.

By eight, the Mulla was back. The cake, now adorned with an elegant, scripted N, was revealed. Nasruddin frowned again:

"I don't like the frosting. Make it pinker. I will pay for the extra trouble."

By eight-thirty, the final version was complete—flawless. The baker, exhausted but proud, reached for a box.

"Hold it," said Nasruddin, planting himself on a chair. "I'm eating it here."

Commentary: Of Taste and Tenacity

At first glance, this seems like a tale of absurd perfectionism. But peer closer and it's classic Nasruddin mischief, blending vanity, consumer entitlement, and comic timing into one rich slice.

The Mulla's insistence on aesthetic excellence—despite his plan to devour the cake immediately—hints at *how often we obsess over presentation even when the outcome is momentary.* Whether it is a speech, a selfie, or a cake, we sometimes value how things *look* more than what they *mean*.

And perhaps there's a gentle jab here too—at the *fickleness of human desire*. What we *think* we want evolves by the hour. What remains constant? The urge to be fussy about frosting.

"Perfection is fleeting. Appetite is eternal."

58

THE DANGERS OF WATER

Mulla Nasruddin's wife was furious—again.

Waving a newspaper at him, she thundered, "Here is another powerful temperance story! Listen to this— 'Young Wilson got into a boat and being intoxicated, upset it, fell into the river and drowned!' See what drink leads to?"

Nasruddin peered over the rim of his glass, calmly asking:

"He fell into the river, right?"

"Yes."

"And he didn't die until he was in the water?"

"That's right."

Nasruddin nodded sagely, took another sip and concluded, "Then it was the water that killed him, not the whisky."

Commentary: Intoxicated Logic

This classic quip is Nasruddin at his deflective best—skewering logic to preserve his indulgence. With comic precision, he shifts the blame from vice to circumstance, making it seem entirely reasonable to fear water more than whisky.

But beneath the laughter lies a deeper truth about *how we justify our attachments*. Whether it's a habit, belief, or bias, humans are endlessly creative in building narratives that support their choices—especially the indulgent ones.

Nasruddin's sly reversal is a perfect example of how clever arguments can sometimes *mask irrational behaviour with the illusion of logic.*

"When reason is drunk, even drowning looks like hydration."

59

THE HONEST THIEF

Every Friday morning, Mulla Nasruddin arrived at the market with a healthy, strong, and excellent donkey—and sold it at a ridiculously low price, far below its market value.

The townsfolk were puzzled, but none dared question a good bargain.

One day, a wealthy donkey-merchant cornered him and grumbled, "Nasruddin, I don't understand. I squeeze every coin—free fodder from farmers, unpaid labour from slaves, yet I cannot match your prices. What's your secret?"

Nasruddin smiled innocently and replied, "Simple. You steal fodder and labour. I merely steal donkeys."

Commentary: When Crime Becomes Comparative

In this razor-sharp satire, Nasruddin lays bare the hypocrisy of *industrialised exploitation* versus petty crime. The rich merchant cloaks his theft under the guise of *efficiency and smart business*, while the Mulla calls a spade a spade—with devastating honesty.

While the audience laughs at the punchline, they are also left with a thorny question:

Is one kind of theft more respectable just because it wears a suit and employs an accountant?

This parable mocks how *systemic injustice hides behind structure and scale*, while individuals like Nasruddin—though technically wrong—expose the absurdity of the moral high ground claimed by the powerful.

"When profit wears perfume, theft smells sweet."

60

THE DONKEY DILEMMA

One day, Mulla Nasruddin and his son set off on a journey. The Mulla, ever thoughtful, let his son ride the donkey while he walked beside.

Soon, they passed a group of travellers. "Look at that selfish boy!" they scoffed. "Riding comfortably while his old father walks in the heat. No respect these days!"

The boy flushed with shame and insisted that his father take the saddle instead.

Not far ahead, another group tut-tutted: "Shame on that father! Look at the poor little boy walking while the old man rides. No compassion!"

So Mulla pulled his son up to ride with him. Moments later, a third crowd gasped:

"Monsters! Two people on one donkey! That poor creature will collapse!"

So, they dismounted and walked beside the donkey.

They had not gone far when they met yet another group. "Idiots!" came the cry. "Both of them walking in this blazing heat while the donkey goes free. That's what comes of education without wisdom!"

Mulla Nasruddin stopped. Then, without a word, he hoisted the donkey onto his shoulders and continued down the path.

"To keep people from talking," he muttered, "this is the only option left."

Commentary: Carrying Burdens That Aren't Yours

This classic gem slices straight through *the human obsession with pleasing others.*

No matter what Nasruddin and his son did—walked, rode, shared, or swapped—someone always had an opinion. In the end, the only way to silence criticism was to do the absurd: carry the donkey.

"He who tries to please everyone ends up looking ridiculous."

The tale is a gentle but piercing reminder:

- Public opinion is as fickle as weather.
- If you constantly adapt your choices to satisfy others, you will eventually carry burdens that were never yours to bear.

"The weight of judgment is heavier than the donkey."

61

COLD LOGIC

Mulla Nasruddin had just tucked himself into bed, cozy and ready for a well-earned night's sleep.

But peace, as always, was a distant dream.

"Mulla," said his wife, "it is cold outside. Get up and shut the window."

He pretended to be asleep.

She repeated: "Mulla, it is freezing. Close the window."

He turned over, eyes shut.

"MULLA NASRUDDIN!" she snapped. "CLOSE THAT WINDOW."

Grumbling in surrender, Nasruddin dragged himself out of bed, shuffled over, slammed the window shut, returned to bed, pulled up the blanket, and with a sigh asked:

"So now… is it warm outside?"

Commentary: The Temperature of Marital Truth

At first glance, this is just another hilarious domestic scene, but hidden in the folds of Nasruddin's blanket lies a gem of insight.

This tale captures:

- The *literalist* in Nasruddin who questions the logic of common sayings.
- The gendered politics of bedtime discomfort.
- And above all, how *doing what you are told does not always mean you agree with it.*

"The outside didn't change—just the argument did."

While Nasruddin *technically* obeys, he also exposes the absurdity of assuming that shutting the window magically changes the weather.

It is his subtle rebellion. He does not mind losing the battle—but he will win a laugh, and sometimes, that is the better victory.

"You can close a window, but you cannot shut down Nasruddin's questions."

62

A HEAD FOR POTATOES

School was out, and little Maksood came storming into the house, sobbing bitterly.

"They beat me up, Dad! The kids said… I have a big head!"

"Now, now," soothed Mulla Nasruddin, "don't listen to them. It is not true. Your head is just fine."

Maksood wiped his tears, somewhat comforted, and went back to school the next day.

That afternoon, the same scene played out. More teasing, more tears.

Again, Nasruddin patted his son on the back. "Forget those kids. They are just being mean. Your head is perfectly normal."

Once Maksood had calmed down, the Mulla said, "Now be a good boy and run down to the store. Get me nine pounds of potatoes."

"Okay, Dad. Give me a bag."

"A bag?" said Nasruddin. "*What for? Carry them in your cap.*"

Commentary: The Unconscious Truth

Poor Maksood. Between bullies at school and a father with *accidental honesty*, the boy never stood a chance!

This tale, while laugh-out-loud funny, serves up a delightful paradox:

- *We try to shield others from painful truths*, but often, our subconscious betrays us.
- Nasruddin means well, but reveals more than intended — proving that sometimes, *your actions scream louder than your reassurances.*

- The story also reminds us that *denial does not reduce the size of the truth*—or in this case, the size of Maksood's noggin.

"A cap big enough to carry nine pounds of potatoes might carry a few pounds of truth too."

This one's a comedic masterstroke in unintentional honesty — with just the right amount of fatherly love and foot-in-mouth wit.

63

THE HARDER JOB: SPEAKING OR LISTENING?

Mulla Nasruddin's wife was running for the state legislature, and it was the final day of a gruelling campaign.

As they returned home late that evening, the Mulla sank into a chair and groaned, "My goodness, I am completely exhausted. I feel like I am about to collapse."

"You? *You are* tired?" exclaimed his wife, removing her campaign sash. "I gave fourteen speeches today!"

"I know," sighed Nasruddin, rubbing his temples. "But *I* had to listen to them."

Commentary: The Unsung Pain of a Good Listener

This laugh-out-loud episode reveals a universal truth—*sometimes, listening is more tiring than talking!*

While his wife thinks she bore the brunt of the campaign, Nasruddin flips the narrative: enduring fourteen speeches as a silent spectator can be its own form of slow torture.

It pokes fun at:

- *The underestimated role of listeners* in relationships and public life.
- The *comic dissonance between effort and endurance*—just because one speaks more doesn't mean the other is not suffering.
- And of course, Nasruddin's unique talent for honesty masked in wit.

"Many speak to be heard. Few listen without losing their minds."

This is a political campaign story where the real vote goes to Nasruddin—for patience and comedic timing!

64

THE HORNS OF A LEGAL DILEMMA

A neighbour approached Mulla Nasruddin seeking clarity on a legal matter.

"My cow was gored by your bull," he said. "Am I entitled to compensation?"

"Certainly not," Nasruddin replied promptly. "How can a man be held responsible for the actions of an animal? That is absurd!"

"Ah," said the neighbour slyly, "I am sorry, I mixed it up. What *actually* happened was that *my* bull gored *your* cow."

Nasruddin raised an eyebrow and said gravely, "Ah… well then, this is more complex. I must consult the *book of precedents*, for there could be *other factors* involved… things that may very well *change* the entire case."

Commentary: When Principles Shift with Perspective

This razor-sharp tale is a satire on *hypocrisy, bias*, and how justice often depends on whose ox is gored—quite literally.

Nasruddin's sudden pivot from certainty to scholarly ambiguity underscores how:

- People *bend the law* to their convenience,
- Self-interest can override consistency,
- And those who hold authority (even if only over a "*book of precedents*") often manipulate interpretation.

"Truth may be blindfolded, but it sees perfectly well who is holding the scale."

This parable invites the reader to laugh—and then reflect on the legal gymnastics and moral relativism that plague both courtrooms and common minds.

65

SIGNED WITH EGO, SEALED WITH WIT

One day, Nasruddin had invited a visiting scholar to his home for a meal.

The scholar arrived at Nasruddin's house, knocked, waited—and knocked again. There was no answer. He looked through the windows. No one.

As the minutes ticked on, the man's self-importance began to boil over.

"Doesn't he know who *I* am?"

"I am *so-and-so*! How *dare* he keep *me* waiting?"

Furious, the scholar grabbed a pencil and furiously scribbled on the door: *"IDIOT!"*

Sometime later, Nasruddin returned home, saw the angry note, and smacked his forehead.

"Oh no! I completely forgot!"

He dashed through the streets until he found the scholar. Panting and apologetic, Nasruddin said, "I'm *so sorry*! I only remembered our appointment when I saw your name written on my door!"

Commentary: When Ego Signs the Register

This delightful story punctures the balloon of *vanity and self-importance*, showing us how humour can be the perfect needle.

Nasruddin's wit turns an insult into an opportunity—reflecting how:

- Offense often comes from inflated ego, not real injury,
- The power of words depends on *interpretation*, not just intention,
- And nothing unsettles arrogance like unexpected humility mixed with humour.

"When someone leaves their ego behind—make sure they don't forget it on *your* doorstep."

This story is a masterclass in how to defuse ego with levity, and how to *win without wounding*.

66

KILLER INSTINCTS AND CLERICAL DUTIES

"I am a bank clerk, Doctor — a quiet family man," said Mulla Nasruddin. "I lead an unblemished life, always contribute to charities, act as sidesman at the mosque… I have nothing to reproach myself with.

Yet I have this strange delusion — I think I am a violent mass murderer. It's ridiculous but deeply disturbing."

The psychiatrist leaned back with a calm smile. "You must not worry," he said reassuringly. "This is quite common — especially among inoffensive, quiet people like you. It is often a mere psychological imbalance."

Then, glancing nervously, he added:

"But before we proceed — *Would you mind lowering that sub-machine gun?*"

Commentary: When Appearances Kill

This riotously absurd tale is a sharp dig at how perception, projection, and politeness can create dangerously funny situations.

Nasruddin appears calm and civil — but his *actions* (and weapon) tell a different story. The psychiatrist, meanwhile, represents the overly rational thinker, trying to explain away clear and present danger with textbook logic.

What it reveals:

- People often ignore the obvious when it clashes with expectations.
- Not all delusions are harmless… especially when armed.
- And sometimes, *those who insist they are harmless may require… further investigation.*

"Do not judge a man by his résumé — check what he is carrying under the coat."

67

REVOLUTIONARY CREAM AND COMPULSION

Mulla Nasruddin lived for the day when the social system would be overturned in a glorious revolution and reshaped to suit his ideals.

"Come the revolution," he declared fervently to his wife, "you will not have to live on bread and potatoes. You will eat strawberries and cream!"

"Actually," replied his wife thoughtfully, "I do not like strawberries and cream."

Mulla's eyes blazed with revolutionary zeal: "*Come the revolution,*" he thundered, "*you will eat strawberries and cream — and you will like it!*"

Commentary: Dictatorship of the Palate

This delightfully absurd exchange offers a sharp jab at *authoritarian idealism* — the kind that claims to liberate but ends up dictating preferences, taste, and even joy itself.

Nasruddin's revolution promises indulgence — but only *his version* of indulgence. It is not about freedom; it is about *imposing a new flavour of control*, now garnished with strawberries.

This tale hints at deeper truths:

- Tyranny isn't always in chains — it can come in spoons of cream.
- What's good for one isn't always good for all.
- *Even revolutions can come with fine print: "Obedience required."*

Beware of any utopia that tells you how to enjoy it.

68

WEDDED BLISS AND POISONED PUFFS

Mulla Nasruddin was sitting in a railway station, peacefully smoking his pipe, when a stern-looking woman sat next to him.

"Sir," she sniffed, "if you were a gentleman, you would not smoke here!"

"Ma'am," said Nasruddin coolly, "if *you* were a lady, you would sit farther away."

The woman fumed but stayed silent for a while. Then she exploded again: "If you were my husband, I would give you poison!"

"Well, Ma'am" said Nasruddin, puffing calmly, "*If you were my wife, I would TAKE IT.*"

Commentary: The War of Wits

This verbal fencing match is a classic duel of sarcasm, and Nasruddin parries every insult with cutting humour. What begins as a self-righteous moral rebuke becomes a comedic battlefield of passive-aggressive banter.

While the woman clings to social etiquette, Nasruddin simply outwits her with unapologetic charm and a devastating comeback.

Lessons wrapped in laughter:

- Being *right* does not mean being *likable.*
- Sarcasm, when sharp, cuts deeper than any sword.
- It is better to be disarmed by wit than armed with rage.

Sometimes, the best smoke is the one that leaves your opponent speechless.

69

SAINTS, SALARIES, AND THE SUIT OF JUSTICE

"I cannot get a job," said Nasruddin, "because I am already in the service of the All-Highest."

"Well then," said his wife, "go and ask Him for your wages—every employer must pay."

Taking her advice, the Mulla went into the garden, knelt, and shouted to the heavens:

"Ya Allah! Send me a hundred gold coins for all my past services. I have been most diligent."

His neighbour, a wealthy moneylender and a prankster overheard him. Wanting to mock Nasruddin, he threw down a bag of exactly 100 gold coins.

Without blinking, Nasruddin picked it up and triumphantly handed it to his wife:

"Behold! Proof that I am a saint. The Lord has paid my salary in full."

Soon enough, the neighbour came demanding his gold back.

"You heard me asking for it," Nasruddin calmly said. "And now you want to take it back? I think not."

The moneylender fumed and dragged him to court.

"I cannot go like this," Nasruddin said. "If I appear in my shabby clothes, the judge may side with you. Lend me your cloak and horse so it appears a fair case."

Eager to win, the man lent him both.

Before the judge, the moneylender spoke first. Then the judge turned to Nasruddin.

"What is your defence?"

"That my neighbour is insane," said the Mulla.

"What proof do you have?"

"Why, just ask him. He will claim that even my horse and cloak are his."

"They *are* mine!" shouted the neighbour.

"CASE DISMISSED," said the judge.

Commentary: When Fools Rush In

This tale is a masterclass in satirical reversal. The moneylender sets out to ridicule Nasruddin's *faith* in divine providence—only to be made the clown in court by his own greed and arrogance.

Nasruddin plays both prophet and prankster. His calm confidence turns the system on its head, and he outwits the very man who tried to outsmart him.

Wit wins where logic fails.

A fool with money is soon parted. A fool with ego? Even faster.

70

THE RECURSIVE SOLUTION

There was once a long-forgotten construction site in town. The workers were gone, but the huge pile of dirt they left behind stayed like an unwanted guest.

The townsfolk did what townsfolk do best—they complained:

"This filth dirties my laundry!"

"Why hasn't the town moved that awful pile?"

"It makes our town look like a beggar's camp!"

Day after day, the complaints piled higher than the dirt.

Mulla Nasruddin, fed up, picked up a spade and started digging a hole nearby. Sure enough, another pile of dirt began to form.

A confused onlooker asked, "Mulla, why are you digging a hole?"

"To bury the dirt, of course," Nasruddin replied, still shovelling away.

"But Hodja, what will you do with *this* new pile of dirt?"

The Mulla glared and snapped, "Do I have to think of *everything* around here?!"

Commentary: When Solutions Multiply the Problem

This parable perfectly captures the flaw in *reactionary problem-solving*—the kind where people rush to fix a problem without ever considering the second-order consequences. The 'quick-fix' and the 'band aid' solution.

Nasruddin mirrors society's reflexive habits: solve problem A by creating problem B, then problem C, until someone finally asks, "*Is this really progress?*"

He also pokes fun at collective inaction. The town had no shortage of complaints, but only Nasruddin picked up a spade—albeit to dig himself into a deeper (literal and metaphorical) hole.

Shifting the dirt doesn't clean the town—it just changes where the dirt lives.

71

THE OTHER SIDE OF THE FENCE

Mulla Nasruddin had been watching a patient at a nearby mental hospital who was busily hammering nails into a fence. What caught his attention, though, was how frequently the man paused, examined a nail, and *angrily threw it away*.

Unable to resist his curiosity, Nasruddin finally asked, "Those nails look perfectly new. Why are you throwing so many away?"

The man scowled, "Because they're defective! Look at this—the points are on the wrong end!"

Nasruddin slapped his forehead and shouted, "You fool! Don't throw them away! ***Those are for the other side of the fence!***"

Commentary: Misfits or Misused?

This tale delivers wisdom with surgical absurdity. What seems like a madman's logic becomes a mirror for *how we discard things—and people—simply because they don't seem to fit.*

The genius of Nasruddin's response lies in its *double irony*:

- First, he takes the lunatic's logic seriously—but *out-logics* it with his own twist.
- Second, he raises a subtle truth: what is useless here might be perfect elsewhere.

Perhaps the problem isn't with the nail—but with our inability to see the other side of the fence.

It is also a reminder that innovation often begins where convention ends—and that sometimes, the *crazy* ones are just misunderstood by those who never flipped their perspective.

72

BETTER YOU SHOULDN'T ASK

Mulla Nasruddin came home after a long, gruelling day at work, collapsed at the kitchen table, and looked at his equally exhausted wife.

"Dear," he said dramatically, "for once in your life, don't begin with your own problems. Ask me instead about my day. Just once, ask what happened to me at work. Go ahead. Ask."

His wife, a bit startled and concerned, hesitantly said, "So… what happened, Mulla?"

Nasruddin groaned, buried his face in his hands, and muttered: "What happened? *Oh, dear… better you should not ask.*"

Commentary: The Drama Within

This story masterfully captures the all-too-human tendency to invite empathy… only to wallow in theatrical self-pity the moment it arrives.

Nasruddin's reaction is hilarious because it is tragically relatable—how often do we *demand to be heard*, only to crumble into complaint when someone actually listens?

It is not always answers we seek; sometimes, we just want someone to ask the question—even if we are not ready to answer it.

Also note the understated brilliance of the wife's role: she is already weary, yet obliges—and gets rewarded with a vague, melodramatic spiral. In Mulla's world, even a conversation can be a trap!

73

P.S. I INSULT YOU

Mulla Nasruddin was sobbing when he opened the door for his wife.

"I have been insulted," he wept. "Your mother insulted me!"

"Mother? But she is a hundred miles away!" his wife exclaimed.

"I know," said Nasruddin, sniffling. "But a letter came for you this morning, and... I opened it."

She looked at him sternly. "That was not meant for you. But where is the insult in that?"

"In the postscript!" said Nasruddin dramatically. "It said: '*Dear Nasruddin, please don't forget to give this letter to my daughter.*'"

Commentary: Thin Skins and Thinner Logic

What makes this story delightful is Nasruddin's artful ability to feel offended—even when the letter wasn't addressed to him, and the postscript was clearly a practical instruction, not an insult.

Sometimes, the human ego is so fragile that even a *harmless reminder* can sound like a *personal affront*—especially if one's guilt or insecurity reads between the lines.

The Mulla, in his infinite absurdity, showcases how *we often twist facts into feelings*, all because we desperately want the world to centre around us—even in a postscript.

74

THE HAT, THE HABIT, AND THE HEAD

Mulla Nasruddin used to sit on the terrace of a certain teahouse. One day, a small boy ran past and knocked his hat off. The Mulla picked it up and said nothing.

The same thing happened again the next day. And the next. And the next. Still, Nasruddin simply dusted off his hat and put it back on.

A friend who watched this repeatedly asked, "Mulla, why don't you catch the boy or ask someone else to teach him a lesson? He is just a child."

"That's not how this works," said Nasruddin, cryptically.

One day, Nasruddin arrived late to the teahouse. In his usual place sat a fearsome-looking soldier wearing a grand fur cap.

Just then, the small boy showed up, as usual. Out of sheer habit, he ran by and knocked the soldier's cap off.

Without missing a beat, the soldier drew his sword and cut off the boy's head—then calmly resumed sipping his tea.

"You see what I mean?" said Nasruddin, turning to his stunned friend.

Commentary: Patience, Power, and the Punchline of Karma

Nasruddin's silence was not cowardice—it was foresight disguised as forbearance. Instead of acting out of anger, he let the world do its own balancing act. And when it did, it was *swift, brutal, and poetic.*

There's a deeper truth here: when a pattern persists, and it seems harmless—don't be fooled. One day, a different player may change the game entirely.

Nasruddin shows that patience is not always passive—*sometimes it is just waiting for the right actor to take the stage.*

75

THE ONE-NOTE WONDER

Once, Mulla Nasruddin bought himself a violin. With great enthusiasm, he picked it up and began to play.

NEEEEEEEEEEEEEEEEEEEEEEEEEEEEEEEEEE...

Same note. Same string. Again. And again. And again.

NEEEEEEEEEEEEEEEEEEEEEEEEEEEEEEEEEE...

Hours passed. His wife, nearly losing her mind, finally screamed, "Nasruddin!"

NEEE...

He stopped. "Yes, dear?"

"Why do you play the same note over and over? Real violinists move their fingers, use other strings! Why don't you play like them?"

Nasruddin calmly replied, "Well, dear, I know why they go up and down the strings..."

"And why is that?"

"They're still looking for *this* note." He raised his bow, and resumed:

NEEEEEEEEEEEEEEEEEEEEEEEEEEEEEEEEEE...

Commentary: The Difference Between Obsession and Mastery

In classic Nasruddin fashion, what sounds like nonsense is a *mirror to human folly*.

Many chase complexity, thinking that variety alone equals value. But Nasruddin champions depth over breadth, even if it sounds a bit... monotonous.

It is a humorous jab at those who pretend sophistication by moving a lot without purpose, while also poking fun at the smugness of the one-trick experts.

You can almost hear him whisper:

"Why fumble for a hundred notes... when I have already found the best one?"

76

BON APPÉTIT, MONSIEUR NASRUDDIN!

Mulla Nasruddin was indulging in a rare luxury—a cruise—and found himself seated at the same dining table as a refined French gentleman.

At their very first meal, the Frenchman greeted him cheerfully with, *"Bon appétit!"*

Polite as ever, Nasruddin replied, "*Mulla Nasruddin.*"

At the next meal, again: "Bon appétit," said the Frenchman. "Mulla Nasruddin," replied the Mulla.

This curious ritual went on for three whole days. Nasruddin, increasingly annoyed, confided in a fellow passenger: "Every time we sit to eat, he says his name is *Bon Appétit*, and I say mine is *Mulla Nasruddin*. Then we repeat it all over again at the next meal!"

The fellow traveller laughed. "No, no, Mulla. *Bon appétit* isn't his name—it means '*enjoy your meal*' in French!"

A wave of relief washed over Nasruddin.

The very next morning at breakfast, feeling worldly and confident, Mulla Nasruddin greeted his tablemate: "Bon appétit!"

To which the Frenchman smiled, nodded politely, and replied: "Mulla Nasruddin."

Commentary: When Manners Meet Misunderstanding

Nasruddin's tale here is not just a classic case of lost in translation, but also a reminder of how:

- *Language without context is often meaningless*, and
- Sometimes we respond out of habit, not comprehension.

What makes it delightful is how *both* parties end up mirroring each other, each believing they are being perfectly polite.

True to Nasruddin's spirit, the story reminds us: *it is better to laugh at our misunderstandings than be embarrassed by them.*

77

NOW THAT'S WHAT I CALL LIVING!

Mulla Nasruddin and his wife were walking through town when a grand funeral procession passed them by. It had everything—a long, polished hearse, luxurious cars laden with fresh flowers, and a seemingly endless parade of mourners.

Nasruddin's wife, impressed but contemplative, remarked,

"It must be some rich fellow. I have seen such funerals before: a solid mahogany casket with gold handles, satin lining, a grand mausoleum with statues, stone doors, prayers, and even a full choir."

Eyes wide, Mulla Nasruddin nodded enthusiastically. "Wow!" he said with admiration.

"Now that's what I call living!"

Commentary: Death with a Touch of Irony

Nasruddin's misplaced admiration nails the paradox of modern life: we spend our entire lives chasing symbols of wealth, luxury, and status—only to be surrounded by them in death, when we no longer care.

In true Mulla fashion, his accidental wit reveals an uncomfortable truth:

We often confuse appearances with living and forget that *living well* has little to do with how we *leave* the world.

This story is a humorous nudge to question: *Are we investing in a rich life or just an expensive departure?*

78

CLOSET CASE: A LEG UP ON PANIC

Mulla Nasruddin arrived late at the country club dance and, in the icy scramble to get inside, slipped and tore a sizeable hole in his trousers.

"Come into the ladies' dressing room," said his ever-practical wife. "There is no one there—I will pin it up for you."

On closer inspection, however, the rip was far too dramatic for a simple pin. Fortunately, a maid provided a needle and thread and stood guard at the door while Mulla removed his trousers and Mrs. Nasruddin got to work with practiced hands.

Just then, there came frantic voices from the hallway.

"We must come in!" a woman cried. "Mrs. Jones is ill!"

Thinking quickly, Mrs. Nasruddin shoved her trouserless husband into a nearby closet.

But a moment later, there was a terrible commotion—thuds, yells, and a familiar voice shouting in panic.

Mrs. Nasruddin froze. "The women are here!" she whispered.

"OH, DAMN THE WOMEN!" came Nasruddin's despairing cry. *"I AM OUT IN THE BALLROOM!"*

Commentary: Between Stitch and Showstopper

This is vintage Nasruddin—caught not just with his pants down, but with comic timing that lands squarely in the absurd.

The scenario exposes the human impulse to manage emergencies with hasty, often ill-conceived solutions. In their frantic effort to avoid embarrassment, the Nasruddins end up *creating* the very scene they were trying to prevent—proving that panic often opens the wrong door (literally and metaphorically).

There's also a deeper social undertone here: a nod to the farcical rigidity of societal norms about decency and gendered spaces. Ironically, Nasruddin's loudest fall wasn't on the icy pavement but into the public gaze—pants less and proud.

Sometimes, when you're hiding from trouble, trouble moves the curtain.

79

THE HOLY HALWA HEIST

Mulla Nasruddin once donned a Sufi robe and set out on a pious pilgrimage. On the way, he met a priest and a yogi, and the trio decided to journey together.

When they arrived at a village, the priest and yogi assigned Nasruddin to collect alms while they meditated and offered prayers. Dutifully, Nasruddin went around and managed to gather a modest sum, with which he bought a bowl of fragrant, delicious halwa.

"I suggest we divide it now," said the Mulla.

"Not yet," said the priest. "It is better to delay gratification."

"Yes," added the yogi. "Let us eat at night, after our spiritual practices."

Come nightfall, Mulla Nasruddin claimed the first portion, arguing, "I was the one who fetched the funds."

"Unacceptable," countered the priest. "As a representative of a structured religious order, I outrank you."

"And I," said the yogi solemnly, "eat only once every three days. Spiritually speaking, I deserve more."

So, they agreed: each would recount their dreams the next morning, and whoever had the most divine vision would get first claim.

In the morning, the priest began:

"I dreamt of the founder of my faith. He raised his hand in benediction and declared me specially chosen."

The yogi followed: "I dreamt I reached Nirvana. I became one with the void, utterly absorbed in eternal silence."

Then they turned to Nasruddin, who burped contentedly and said:

"I dreamt that Khidr, the great guide of saints, appeared and said, 'Nasruddin, arise at once and eat the halwa!' Naturally, I had to obey."

Commentary: Dream On, While I Dine

This tale is a delectable example of Nasruddin's divine cheek—and razor-sharp logic. The story plays with the lofty claims of religious superiority, the illusion of self-importance cloaked in piety, and the human tendency to delay action in pursuit of abstract rewards.

Nasruddin, meanwhile, keeps it simple: the halwa was real, the hunger was real, and dreams are best served with dessert already eaten.

The lesson?

While others debate in dreams, the wise one wakes—and finishes the halwa.

In other words: *Spirituality is fine, but do not let it come between you and dessert.*

80

THE FRIDAY FIASCO AND THE KNOW-IT-ALL CROWD

Once, the good citizens of a city invited Mulla Nasruddin to deliver the Friday *khutba* (sermon). Climbing up the minbar, the Mulla looked around at the blank faces and opened with a question:

"Do you know what I am going to say?"

The congregation replied in unison, "NO!"

Nasruddin sniffed, "Well then, I have no desire to speak to people who do not even know what I will be talking about," and promptly walked off the pulpit.

Embarrassed and confused, the people invited him again the following Friday. This time, when Nasruddin asked, "Do you know what I am going to say?" they all responded, "YES!"

"Excellent," he said, "Since you already know, I will not waste your time," and again, he left.

Now deeply puzzled, they invited him a third time. When Nasruddin asked the same question, the crowd had prepared a clever trick. Half of them shouted "YES" and the other half, "NO."

Without missing a beat, Nasruddin smiled and said: "Good. Then the half who know what I am going to say should explain it to the other half!"

And with that, he walked off triumphantly once more.

Commentary: When in Doubt, Let the Crowd Teach Itself

This tale is a masterclass in wit, crowd psychology, and the subtle art of avoiding responsibility—all rolled into one sermon with zero effort.

Nasruddin flips the audience's expectations three times, and in doing so, exposes their habit of either blind agreement or unthinking disagreement. He uses their own answers to elude every obligation—and turns the whole ordeal into a teaching moment.

The deeper wisdom?

Do not expect clarity from a confused crowd. And if you are not ready for the answer, do not ask a Sufi the question.

Or more succinctly: *When half the crowd is clueless, it is best to let them educate one another—especially if you would rather go home for lunch.*

81

THE INFINITE APPETITE AND THE ILLUSION OF SLICES

In Birmingham, Mulla Nasruddin stayed as a lodger at a kind landlady's house. Wanting to keep him content, she began by packing him a modest lunch: just two slices of bread.

The next evening, she noticed the Mulla wasn't quite pleased. So, the following day, she gave him four slices. Still not satisfied. The day after that—six. And then eight. Finally, *ten slices* of bread, but Nasruddin's expression remained as dry as the sandwich.

Out of both pity and pantry ideas, she sliced an *entire loaf in half*, put butter in between, and packed it up neatly for him.

That evening, she eagerly asked, "Had you enough today, Mulla?"

Mulla Nasruddin frowned slightly and said:

"It was not bad… but I see you are back to the two slices again."

Commentary: When Perception Trumps Proportion

The Mulla's logic defies arithmetic, but not reality. His hunger wasn't just for bread—it was for *visible growth*. The moment the slice count appeared to diminish, even symbolically, he perceived lack, no matter the actual content.

This story is a reminder that *humans often measure satisfaction not by substance, but by symbols*—the size of the slice, the number of likes, the weight of the title, or the thickness of the envelope.

In today's terms:

"If your progress isn't obvious, someone will always think you are slipping—even if you have got the whole loaf."

Or as Nasruddin would put it:

"Never underestimate the power of optical portioning."

82

THE ELEPHANT DEAL YOU CAN'T REFUSE

One fine day, Mahmood caught up with Mulla Nasruddin and made him an offer that only a lunatic or a legend would entertain.

"Nasruddin, I've got a bargain for you! A whole elephant—alive, large, and only one thousand rupees!"

Nasruddin looked at him incredulously.

"Are you crazy? What do I want with an elephant?"

Mahmood persisted.

"It is a beautiful creature. All grey. Ten feet tall. Complete trunk."

Nasruddin threw his arms up.

"But I have got *nowhere* to put it. I live in a three-room walk-up on the sixth floor!"

Mahmood leaned in, adding,

"Two beautiful tusks—two feet long each. A majestic beast. They don't make them like that anymore."

Nasruddin shrieked,

"I cannot feed it, I cannot house it, I don't need it!"

Mahmood thought for a second and then said:

"Okay, Nasruddin, *you drive a hard bargain.* Tell you what—*I will throw in another elephant for just 100 rupees more.*"

And Mulla Nasruddin, suddenly delighted, said:

"Now you are talking!"

Commentary: When Logic Gets Trampled by a Bargain

In the world of haggling and hype, *value often overrides viability*. Nasruddin's sudden shift from *no use at all* to *now you're talking* wasn't based on utility—it was based on ***perceived deal value***.

He did not need a single elephant, but he was willing to pay more for two. Why?

Because *the allure of a "great bargain" can short-circuit practical thinking*.

This story is a hilarious commentary on how even the wisest among us can get trapped by the psychological lure of *more for less*.

In today's language: *"Buy one useless thing, get a second useless thing half off—and feel like a genius."*

Or, as Mulla might say: "I may not need it, but I would be a fool to pass up two!"

83

DOUBTFUL, NOT DANGEROUS

Mulla Nasruddin, running for public office, was canvassing the countryside with his young son. He had a clever system: his son would keep index cards to record whether each voter was for or against him.

As they pulled up to one farmhouse, a furious farmer stormed out the door *with a shotgun.*

"I know who you are, you good-for-nothing crook! You deserve to be in jail. Don't even think about stepping inside that gate or I will blow your head off! Now scram before I lose my temper and make a mess I will regret!"

Nasruddin quickly obeyed and sped off with his son.

After a few minutes of tense silence, the boy, flipping through his cards, asked:

"Well, Father... I guess I should tear up that man's card?"

To which Mulla replied with indignation:

"Tear it up?! Certainly not. Just mark him down as doubtful."

Commentary: The Power of Perspective (and Denial)

This classic tale oozes with Mulla's characteristic optimism—or is it *delusional hope*? While the average politician might see a shotgun-wielding threat as a lost cause, Nasruddin remains unflinchingly pragmatic (and hilariously detached from reality).

His logic? *If he didn't actually get shot, there is still a chance.*

It is a brilliant take on the *twisted optimism of campaigners*, who refuse to write anyone off—even those who want to *write them off the face of the earth.*

In modern-day parlance:

"Just because someone hates you, threatens your life, and calls you a crook does not mean they will not vote for you."

A parable of political hope… or political hopelessness.

84

DONKEY-LOGIC DEFEATS THE SAGES

A band of travelling philosophers made it their business to challenge the greatest minds of every town they visited. Their next stop: the hometown of Mulla Nasruddin.

The Governor, having seen his own intellectuals humbled before, summoned Mulla and advised:

"Speak to those who've debated them before. Learn their methods."

But Nasruddin simply said:

"The less I know of their thinking, the better. I do not wish to be imprisoned by their artificialities."

And so, in a grand hall before a large audience, the debate began.

Philosopher 1:
"What is the exact centre of the Earth?"

Nasruddin:
"Where my donkey's hoof is resting right now."

Philosopher:
"Prove it!"

Nasruddin:
"You disprove it. Bring a tape measure."

Philosopher 2:
"How many stars are there in the sky?"

Nasruddin:
"Exactly as many as the hairs on my donkey's coat. Anyone who doubts it may count both."

Philosopher 3:
"How many avenues of human perception are there?"

Nasruddin:
"Equal to the hairs in your beard. I can pluck each hair to demonstrate everyone. Or we could count the hairs in my donkey's tail instead."

Dumbfounded and defeated, the philosophers huddled. They bowed and joined Mulla Nasruddin—not as rivals, but as disciples.

Commentary: When Nonsense Outwits Sophistry

Mulla Nasruddin's genius lies not in complex arguments, but in cutting through pretension with *irreverent logic*. While the philosophers sought precision and pedantry, the Mulla revealed that *truth without common sense is just noise wrapped in robes.*

By answering absurdity with equal absurdity, Nasruddin showed:

"Sometimes the smartest response is not to play the game—but to change the board entirely."

And if truth is relative, then so are donkey hairs.

85

THE POWER OF UNINTELLIGIBLE WISDOM

A wise old sage from distant *Ashsharq* arrived in Nasruddin's village, spouting such profound philosophy that the tea-house regulars were dazzled and deferential.

Mulla Nasruddin listened with the air of one unimpressed.

"You know," he said to the robed visitor, "I have had experiences much like yours—I, too, have been a wandering teacher."

The old man bristled. "Tell me, if you *must*."

"Oh, I must," said the Mulla. "I travelled through Kurdistan. Wherever I went—monasteries, caravanserais, tea-houses—I was welcomed. People admired me. Hung on to every word."

Growing visibly irked, the sage snapped, "Did *nobody* ever object to anything you said?"

"Oh, yes. Once, I was beaten, put in the stocks, and thrown out of town."

"Why?"

"Well, that town spoke Turkish. And I was teaching in Turkish."

"Then how did you manage to teach everywhere else?"

"Oh, that is easy," said Nasruddin. "The people who admired me were all Kurds. They had no idea what I was saying."

Commentary: Admiration Often Rests on Ambiguity

This story is a sharp jab at the hollow grandeur of *incomprehensible jargon* and the blind reverence it inspires. Mulla Nasruddin understood that when no one understands you, they might assume you are wise. But clarity, on the other hand, risks scrutiny—and consequences.

"Sometimes it is not your message that matters, but your audience's inability to comprehend it."

In a world where eloquence is often mistaken for insight, the Mulla's wit reminds us that *truth without understanding is as useless as poetry to a stone.*

86

GRAVE MISUNDERSTANDINGS

One lonely evening, while walking down a deserted road, Mulla Nasruddin spotted a group of horsemen approaching at speed.

His imagination—always eager to overwork—went wild: *They are bandits!* he thought. *They will rob me, beat me, kill me!*

Panicked, he scrambled over a wall into a graveyard and flung himself into an open grave to hide.

The horsemen—ordinary travellers with no villainous intent—watched this odd behaviour in confusion. Out of concern, they followed him and found him lying stiff in the grave, eyes wide with fear.

"What on earth are you doing?" they asked. "We saw you run and hide. Can we help? Why are you in a grave?"

Nasruddin, now slightly embarrassed but ever philosophical, replied:

"Just because you ask a question does not mean there's a simple answer. It all depends on your point of view. But if you insist… *I am here because of you—and you are here because of me*!"

Commentary: Fear Paints Shadows Where None Exist

This classic Nasruddin tale skewers our tendency to act on imaginary dangers. His response—witty yet layered—turns the tables on reality:

"I feared you for no reason. But my fear made you chase me. So, who really caused what?"

It is a reminder that *assumptions, once acted upon, can create the very reality we were trying to avoid.*

When fear becomes your guide, even friendly strangers can look like enemies—and an open grave like a haven.

87

NOT MY SHIP, NOT MY STORM

Once, Mulla Nasruddin was aboard a ship making a long journey across the sea.

Midway, a terrible storm rolled in. The winds howled, waves crashed, and chaos erupted. The ship groaned and tilted violently. Crew members scrambled to lower lifeboats. Passengers shrieked, prayed, or fainted.

But amidst this apocalypse-at-sea, Mulla Nasruddin sat quietly on a coil of rope, calm as a monk at sunrise, humming a little tune to himself.

A frantic friend shouted, "Mulla! How can you be so calm? Can't you see the ship is sinking?"

Nasruddin shrugged and replied with perfect composure:

"So? The ship is not my property."

Commentary: When Detachment Becomes Disassociation

On the surface, this is classic Nasruddin absurdity—finding tranquillity in the middle of a shipwreck, simply because *he doesn't own the ship*. But as with most Nasruddin tales, the joke hides a deeper jab.

Is Nasruddin modelling Zen-like detachment—or dangerous denial?

There is a fine line between *non-attachment and irresponsibility*. Sometimes, being too philosophical can be a way of avoiding action. The storm affects everyone, regardless of who owns the vessel.

It is as if the Mulla is saying:

"If it is not mine, it's not my problem."

Which, in today's world—be it climate change, global warming, politics, or public health—is exactly the kind of thinking that sinks us all.

88

THE GOOD SAMARITAN... WHO COULDN'T TAKE A HINT

Nasruddin, who fancied himself a night-time saviour of drunks and derelicts, was taking a late walk when he noticed a man slumped against the entrance of an apartment building.

"What is the matter?" asked the Mulla. "Drunk?"

"Yup."

"You live here?"

"Yup."

"Want help getting upstairs?"

"Yup."

So, Mulla half-dragged, half-hoisted the man up the stairs. "Which floor?"

"Yup," the man said again, helpfully.

Deciding he must mean the second floor, Mulla opened the nearest door, shoved the man in, and walked back down.

In the vestibule, another man sat in an even worse state.

"Drunk?"

"Yep."

"You live here?"

"Yep."

"Want help upstairs?"

"Yep."

Same story. Same second floor. Same door. Mulla deposited him with a groan.

But as he reached the entrance again, he spotted yet another staggering man. This time, the poor soul caught sight of Nasruddin and flung himself into the arms of a policeman.

"Officer! For heaven's sake, save me!" he cried.

"That man has done nothing all night but carry me upstairs and throw me down the elevator shaft!"

Commentary: When Good Intentions Go Repeatedly Unexamined

Nasruddin meant well. But he failed to question the outcomes of his actions—even when they got increasingly absurd. His *helping* became harming, and yet he persisted.

The road to hell is paved with assumptions.

This story is a reminder that "one-size-fits-all kindness" can quickly become a farce when we forget to check whether our solutions actually suit the situation—or the person.

And sometimes… The best way to *help someone stand up* is to stop picking them up in the wrong way.

89

HOT AIR AND COLD LOGIC

A man—erudite, experienced, and ever so convinced of his own cleverness—decided he would *finally* learn from Mulla Nasruddin. "Surely," he thought, "even madness must have a method. I have studied with gurus, debated with philosophers, and outwitted logicians. This Nasruddin will not fool me."

After a long and weary journey, he reached the Mulla's humble home perched on a windswept mountain ledge. Peering through the window, he saw Nasruddin blowing into his cupped hands beside a weak fire.

Once inside, the man asked, "What are you doing?"

"Warming my hands with my breath," said Nasruddin simply.

Later, when Nasruddin's wife served them both hot broths, the visitor watched as the Mulla blew on it again.

"What are you doing now?" he asked, trying to decipher this contradiction.

"Cooling the broth with my breath," said Nasruddin.

The man's scholarly mind almost exploded.

"The man is clearly a fraud," he thought. "First, he blows to warm, now he blows to cool. This is no sage—this is a charlatan!"

And he left, sneering at the mountain wind. But on the way down, he told himself,

"At least I learned something today… *that Nasruddin is not a teacher worth learning from.*"

Commentary: It is Not the Wind, It is Your Understanding

The breath is the same. The effect depends on *context*—proximity, temperature, medium.

The visitor brought with him a rigid mindset, looking for *consistency in symbols*, not meaning in function. He missed the wisdom not because it wasn't there—but because he did not know how to recognize it.

This story is a humorous jab at intellectual arrogance. *When you approach wisdom thinking you already know its form, you are blind to its essence.*

Sometimes, Mulla's hot air is the *coolest* lesson you'll get.

90

A POETIC MISFIRE

One fine morning, Mulla Nasruddin flipped through a magazine and came across a quaint little poem:

Sir, why not buy a bunch or two
Of springtime flowers fair?
And take them home one cheerless day,
But carry them with care.
Just hand them to your wife and say,
"I thought of you in town today."

Nasruddin was moved. His heart swelled. His romantic instincts—dormant for years—were stirred into noble action. "Why not?" he said aloud, and off he went.

He returned with a beautiful bouquet of flowers. Instead of simply walking in, he rang the bell with ceremony. His wife opened the door, her hair frayed, her eyes puffy.

Wordlessly, with flair and finesse, he handed her the bouquet.

To his utter surprise, she *burst into tears.*

"Whatever is the matter?" Nasruddin asked, flustered.

Between sobs, she wailed,

"I broke the teapot, the baby hasn't stopped crying, the cook just quit... and now you come home *drunk*!"

Commentary: When Timing Trumps Intention

The poem was perfect. The gesture was sincere. The flowers were fragrant. But the context? *A total disaster.*

Sometimes, when you break character in a moment of poetic spontaneity, people *suspect the worst.* Especially if your usual greeting is "What is for dinner?" and today it is "Darling, I thought of you."

This tale is a reminder that *sudden virtue can look suspicious when it is not habitual.*

Or at least… take off your tipsy grin before handing over the roses.

91

BULLISH ROMANCE AND A CANDID WARNING

A love-struck young man was out for a countryside drive with his sweetheart. Eager to impress her with some rustic charm, he pulled over, leapt over a fence, and trotted into a field to pluck a bouquet of wildflowers.

He was mid-pick, envisioning her swooning over his floral offering, when he noticed a *snort* behind him. Then another. He turned.

There, not ten feet away, stood **a massive bull**—horns arched, head lowered, one hoof scraping the earth with escalating fury.

Frozen in panic, the youth spotted a man leaning lazily on the far fence. It was Mulla Nasruddin, the owner of the field.

"Hey!" the young man shouted. "Is that bull *safe*?"

Nasruddin shaded his eyes, examined the scene with calm detachment, and replied:

"Safe as anything…"

Then, after a thoughtful pause, he added:

"…Cannot say the same about *you*, though!"

Commentary: Bull-headed Bravery vs. Pasture Protocol

The young swain sought romance among the wildflowers—but forgot to factor in the wildlife.

Nasruddin's dry reply perfectly captures the essence of wisdom wrapped in wit. *The bull was safe—from legal liability, perhaps. But not from the laws of nature.*

In life, many things are safe in theory. But *safety is not always a shared agreement between you and the universe*—especially if you are on the wrong end of a horn.

So next time you step into someone else's field, maybe check with the *bull* first.

Or bring flowers from a shop. Preferably one *not guarded by livestock*.

92

THE COBWEB, THE CANVAS, AND A TOUCH OF CYNICISM

"One day," said Mulla Nasruddin's wife with admiration, "I knew an artist who painted a cobweb on the ceiling so realistically, the maid spent hours trying to get it down."

Nasruddin did not even look up from his tea. "Sorry, dear," he said flatly. "I just do not believe it."

"Why not?" she asked indignantly. "Artists do such things all the time. You always doubt everything I say!"

Nasruddin nodded slowly and replied:

"Yes, artists I can believe. But *maids* putting in *hours* to clean something? THAT, my dear, defies all known laws of nature."

Commentary: Art Imitates Life, But Does Life Really Clean?

Nasruddin's quick wit once again takes a detour from the obvious. While the story was meant to marvel at artistic brilliance, he steers it straight into the realm of domestic scepticism.

Rather than question the talent of the artist, he questions the *motivation of the maid*, hinting at a certain universal truth: *sometimes, the most unbelievable part of a tale is not the masterpiece—it is the people around it.*

As always, Nasruddin does not just *doubt*, he *dismantles* the narrative—with comic precision.

93

A PRAYER FOR ALL POSSIBILITIES

A theologian lay ill, teetering between life and death. In his fevered haze, he remembered tales of Mulla Nasruddin—a man rumoured to commune with unseen realms.

"Call him," he said. "Perhaps… there is something to all this mysticism after all."

Nasruddin arrived and leaned close.

"Prescribe me a prayer," whispered the theologian, "something to ease my passage into the next world."

With a warm smile, Nasruddin said,

"Certainly. Here you go: *'God help me — Devil help me!'*"

The theologian bolted upright, scandalized. "Mulla! That is blasphemy! Are you out of your mind?"

Nasruddin shrugged calmly.

"Not at all. At your stage, my friend, it is best not to take chances. When you see two doors, it is wise to knock on both."

Commentary: When Theology Meets Pragmatism

In typical Nasruddin style, this parable skewers the rigid certainty of dogma with the razor of practical wit. Why commit to only one eternal hotline, when you might have dial-up service on both ends?

The Mulla's wisdom is not in impiety—it is in understanding human nature. Faced with the unknown, *certainty often gives way to caution*… or at least hedging your metaphysical bets.

It is not faith he mocks—it is *self-righteousness without humour.*

94

OF BRIDES AND BOVINES

Mulla Nasruddin had a stunning daughter—so beautiful that the village men's eyes nearly fell out every time she walked by. Nasruddin, however, guarded her like a secret recipe, reserving her for a wealthy young khan from just outside the village.

When the khan finally came to propose, the Mulla struck a record-setting bride-price—gold, silver, and perhaps a camel or three. But, with typical ceremony and calculation, he insisted on a long waiting period before the wedding.

What the Mulla didn't know was that his daughter had fallen head over heels for a charming village loafer—the kind who loiters near wells and hearts. Her water-fetching trips stretched into romantic escapades, and soon, the girl was unmistakably with child.

The day of the wedding came. The khan arrived with pomp and pride—only to find his bride visibly pregnant.

Scandalised, he stormed at the Mulla. "What is the meaning of this?! How could this happen?"

Mulla Nasruddin shrugged. "These things are normal after marriage."

The khan exploded, "Then I am calling off the marriage—and I want my down payment back!"

The Mulla scratched his beard and called after him. "Wait, wait—let us be sensible. In fact, now that my daughter is pregnant and will bear you a son, I must *double* the bride price!"

"*Double?!*" gasped the khan. "Why in Allah's name?!"

Mulla Nasruddin calmly replied:

"Just last week, I delivered a cow I had sold months earlier. During the wait, she got pregnant. When I handed her over, I demanded and received double the amount. Now, what is so different between a cow and a daughter?"

Commentary: Dowry, Daughters, and Double Standards

Nasruddin's outrageous logic walks the razor's edge of satire, slicing deep into society's treatment of women as transactional assets.

His final line—comparing daughter to cow—is so scandalously blunt that it forces us to *examine the very premise of bride-price systems.* He holds up a funhouse mirror to traditions that commodify marriage, and through absurdity, exposes their underlying absurdities.

Once again, Nasruddin does not play by the rules. He simply holds them up, turns them inside out—and lets the world gasp in horror or laughter.

95

THE BULL AND THE BURDEN

One sunny morning, a friend of Mulla Nasruddin was stunned to witness a bizarre scene: Nasruddin was out in the field, ploughing his land. But instead of using an ox or a donkey, he had hitched his *prize-winning, twenty-five-thousand-rupee bull* to the plough.

"Mulla!" cried the astonished friend. "Have you lost your mind? That bull is worth a fortune! Why on earth are you making *him* pull a plough?"

Mulla Nasruddin, sweat glistening on his brow and resolve firm in his eyes, replied grimly:

"That bull has won trophies, eaten the best feed, and been paraded around like a king. It is about time he learned that life isn't all play."

Commentary: From Pride to Ploughshare

Nasruddin's lesson here isn't just for livestock—it's a parable for pampered egos, privileged upbringings, and those who believe accolades exempt them from effort. Even champions, the Mulla reminds us, need to stay grounded (*sometimes literally*).

In a world where comfort quickly breeds complacency, Nasruddin's unconventional logic suggests:

"*Let your prize bull pull a plough once in a while—so he remembers what ground feels like beneath his hooves.*"

96

THE MILLIONAIRE'S MORNING

Mulla Nasruddin was lounging under a tree with two of his friends—one a passionate Spaniard, the other an adventurous American—when the conversation drifted into the land of dreams.

"What would you do," asked the Spaniard, "if you woke up tomorrow and discovered you were a millionaire?"

"I would build a grand bullring!" he declared with fire in his eyes.

The American chimed in: "I would head straight to Paris! Wine, women, and the Eiffel Tower—I would spend every dime having the time of my life!"

They both turned to Mulla Nasruddin, expecting a similarly extravagant vision.

The Mulla stroked his beard, yawned, and said:

"I would go right back to sleep—just to see if I could make another million."

Commentary: Dream Big, Snooze Bigger

While others fantasize about spending wealth, Nasruddin flips the script with his classic absurdity. In a single sentence, he jabs at both the pursuit of riches and the futility of wishful thinking unbacked by effort.

Sometimes the real joke lies in how we expect wealth to change our lives—when all it does, perhaps, is inspire us to keep dreaming.

Because in Nasruddin's world, why settle for just *one* million… when you could *sleep* your way to two?

97

THE MERCHANT OF MISERY

A wealthy merchant once spent a few days in Nasruddin's village. Though famously stingy, people greeted him with deep respect every time he passed by.

"Makes no sense," muttered Nasruddin. "Why salute someone who doesn't even flip a copper coin your way?"

A neighbour replied, "You don't get it, Mulla. He is a *merchant*. That counts for something. Who knows, maybe one day, out of the blue, he might actually give us something."

A week after the merchant left, Nasruddin wandered into the village market with a strange gleam in his eye. He bought a dozen watermelons at one stall—then promptly sold them at the next, making a small loss. Then he bought cucumbers and sold them again, this time at a bigger loss.

He repeated this cycle with several items until, dripping in imaginary prestige and quite a few rupees poorer, he strutted into the teahouse.

"Bring me your finest pink tea!" he commanded. "Whip the cream like it owes you money! And toss in some cardamoms for nobility!"

Curious villagers began to gather, whispering about Nasruddin's strange new behaviour.

Finally, someone asked, "Mulla, why are you buying and selling at a loss?"

Nasruddin slammed the teacup on the table and roared:

"How dare you question me! I am a merchant! Isn't that something? And who knows… maybe I will give you something one day!"

Commentary: When Status Is the Product

In this classic satire, Nasruddin mirrors society's absurd deference to wealth—even when the wealthy are of no benefit to anyone but themselves. He exposes the blind respect afforded to titles without substance and reminds us: *status without generosity is just theatre.*

After all, if all it takes to be respected is *pretending to be rich*—then why not lose money in style?

98

THE POT THAT LIVED AND DIED

Nasruddin once rode into town backwards on his donkey.

"Why are you sitting like that, Mulla?" asked the townsfolk.

"I know where I am going," he replied. "But it is where I have been that concerns me!"

That same evening, Nasruddin walked over to his neighbour's house and said, "Friend, may I borrow a pot? I promise to return it tomorrow."

The neighbour obliged.

The next day, Nasruddin returned the pot—along with a smaller one inside.

"What's this?" asked the puzzled neighbour.

"Oh," said Nasruddin with a wink, "your pot gave birth."

Overjoyed at his unexpected gain, the neighbour thanked him profusely.

A few days later, Nasruddin came again, asking to borrow a much *larger* pot. With greed now outweighing caution, the neighbour happily handed it over.

A week passed. Then another. No sign of Nasruddin or his pot.

One day, the neighbour ran into him at the bazaar. "Mulla, what happened to my pot?"

Nasruddin looked sorrowful and said, "Ah… I did not want to be the one to tell you, but—it died."

"Died?! How can a pot die?"

"Well," said Nasruddin, "if it can give birth… surely it can die too."

Commentary: When Greed Overrules Reason

This tale is a gleaming double-edged sword. On one side, Nasruddin holds a mirror to *human gullibility driven by greed.* On the other, he uses absurd logic to expose how easily people accept lies when they serve self-interest—but protest when they face loss.

We rarely question a miracle—so long as we profit from it. But the same logic we accept with joy, we reject in despair.

99

CROOKED STAIRS AND CROOKED TIMING

Abdul Rehman was gravely ill, and his friends began taking turns to visit and keep his spirits high. On one such evening, it was Mulla Nasruddin's turn.

He was given strict instructions: "Whatever you do, Mulla, do not say anything discouraging. He is very low."

Mulla agreed. When he entered, he put on his brightest smile, cracked a few jokes, and even had Rehman chuckling. Spirits were lifting. All was going well—until Nasruddin suddenly paused and began shaking his head solemnly.

Rehman, alarmed, asked, "What is it, Mulla? Why are you frowning?"

Nasruddin sighed deeply and said, "I was just thinking… how in the name of the Holy Prophet are they ever going to get a coffin down the crooked stairs of this house?"

Commentary: A Sense of Timing More Terminal Than the Patient

This tale reminds us of Nasruddin's unmatched ability to blend empathy with absurdity. His concern may have been practical—but his timing was mortally inappropriate.

Even when trying to be helpful, Nasruddin cannot resist *taking the wrong turn—especially down a crooked staircase of thought.*

100

THE CHICKENS, THE CAKE, AND THE CURIOUS DISCIPLE

Hardly anyone could understand Mulla Nasruddin. At times he snatched victory from the jaws of defeat; at others, he sabotaged success with absurd blunders. Still, rumours swirled that he lived on an entirely different plane of existence.

A curious young man, determined to uncover Nasruddin's secrets, decided to spy on him.

He followed the Mulla to a quiet riverbank, where Nasruddin sat under a tree, seemingly doing nothing. But suddenly, the Mulla stretched out his hand—*and a cake appeared!* He ate it. He repeated the gesture twice more, and three cakes vanished into his belly. Then he reached out again and drank from an invisible goblet that appeared out of thin air.

Stunned, the youth ran up and grabbed Nasruddin's arm. "Tell me how you do these things! I will do anything you ask!"

Nasruddin nodded sagely. "You must first get into the right state of mind—where time and space are meaningless. Only then can you reach out and be handed sweetmeats from the Sultan's chamberlain himself."

The young man eagerly agreed to any conditions.

"Would you like the easy path or the difficult one?" asked Nasruddin.

"The difficult one!" shouted the youth.

"Ah," sighed Nasruddin, "then you've already made your first mistake."

Nasruddin continued, "Here is your first exercise: Make a hole in your fence large enough for your chickens to get into your neighbour's garden, but small enough so that his chickens cannot get into yours."

The young man was flummoxed. He spent days trying to design this magical one-way hole—but failed. He never returned to Nasruddin.